CLASSIC CHINESE COOKING

A QUANTUM BOOK

Published by Chartwell Books
A Division of Book Sales, Inc.
114 Northfield Avenue
Edison, New Jersey 08837
USA

ISBN 0-7858-0644-X

This book was produced by
Quantum Books Ltd
6 Blundell Street
London N7 9BH

Produced in Australia by Griffin Colour

CLASSIC
CHINESE
COOKING

CHARTWELL
BOOKS, INC.

◆ SOUPS ◆

GOOD STOCK

SERVES 12

3–4lb chicken (broiler if available) or
*   duck carcass or spareribs*
Scant 4½ pints water
3–4 slices fresh ginger root

Remove the breast meat and the 2 legs from the chicken. Boil the remaining carcass of the chicken in 3¾ pints water for 20 minutes. Remove from the heat and add ⅔ cup cold water. (The adding of the cold water causes the fat and impurities to cling together, making them easier to remove.) Skim the surface of all scum which rises to the top. Add the ginger and continue to simmer gently for about 1½ hours. After about an hour of simmering, remove the chicken carcass from the stock. Mince the leg meat and the breast meat separately. Add the leg meat to the stock at this stage. Simmer for 10 minutes, then add the breast meat and simmer for about 5 minutes. Strain the stock through a fine strainer or cheesecloth.

DOUBLE-BOILED PIGEON, HAM AND
BLACK MUSHROOM SOUP

DOUBLE-BOILED PIGEON, HAM AND BLACK MUSHROOM SOUP

SERVES 4–6

2 pigeons or squab
8oz lean pork
6 medium black mushrooms
1½oz ham
3 slices fresh ginger root
1tbsp Chinese yellow wine
2½ cups chicken stock
3–4tbsp oil

Clean the pigeons thoroughly. Cut out the breast meat and save it for a stir-fried supreme of pigeon. Blanch the lean pork and pigeons in boiling water for 2 minutes and rinse under the tap for 1 minute. Soak the black mushrooms in warm water for about 30 minutes until they have softened. Discard the stems and cut the caps into evenly sized pieces.

Put all the ingredients in a heavy pot or casserole with a lid, add the stock and an equal amount of water, and cover and steam over medium heat for 3 hours. Double boiling is the favorite Cantonese way of preparing soup. The Cantonese believe that it not only makes the flavor richer but increases the nutritional value.

DRIED TOFU SKIN AND VERMICELLI SOUP

SERVES 4–6

½oz dried tofu skin
1oz golden needles (dried, tiger-lily buds)
¼oz black moss
2oz bean thread vermicelli
4 cups water
1tsp salt
3tbsp light soy sauce

◆ SOUPS ◆

1tbsp rice wine or dry sherry
1tsp fresh ginger root, finely chopped
2 green onions, finely chopped
2tsp sesame seed oil
fresh cilantro to garnish

Soak the tofu skin in hot water for 30–35 minutes and then cut it into small pieces. Soak the lily buds and black moss in water separately for about 20–25 minutes. Rinse the lily buds until clean. Loosen the black moss until it resembles human hair.

With a pair of scissors, cut the vermicelli into short lengths.

Bring the water to a boil in a wok or large pot, and add all the ingredients together with the seasonings. Stir until well blended. Cook the soup for 1–1½ minutes. Add the sesame seed oil and serve hot, garnished with cilantro.

DRIED TOFU SKIN AND VERMICELLI SOUP

DUCK AND CABBAGE SOUP

SERVES 4–6

1 duck carcass (plus giblets if available)
1lb Chinese cabbage
2 slices fresh ginger root
salt and Sichuan pepper

Break up the carcass, place it together with the giblets and any other bits and pieces in a large pot or pan; cover it with water, add the root ginger, bring it to a boil. Skim off the impurities floating on the surface and let it simmer gently with a lid on for at least 45 minutes

About 20 minutes before serving, add the washed and sliced cabbage. Season, then serve.

BEEF BROTH TOMATO SOUP

SERVES 4–6

3oz lean beef
1½tsp salt
2tbsp cornstarch
½ egg white
5tbsp vegetable oil
6 firm medium tomatoes
2 green onions
2½ pints good stock (see recipe)
3–4 slices fresh ginger root
1 chicken stock cube
1½tbsp light soy sauce
pepper to taste
1 egg
1tsp sesame seed oil

Cut the beef into very thin slices. Rub with the salt and cornstarch, then toss in the egg white. Heat the vegetable oil in a wok or skillet. When moderately hot, gently fry the beef for 30 seconds, then drain. Cut each tomato into 6 pieces. Cut onions into ½ inch sections.

Bring the stock to a boil in a wok or saucepan. Add the ginger, crumbled stock cube, beef, soy sauce, pepper, green onion and tomatoes. Simmer for 2 minutes and then pour the beaten egg into the soup in a thin stream. Finally, add the sesame seed oil. Stir and serve immediately.

◆ SOUPS ◆

◆ SOUPS ◆

BEAN SPROUT SOUP

SERVES 4–6

8oz fresh bean sprouts
1 small red bell pepper, cored and seeded
3tbsp oil
2tsp salt
2½ cups water
1 green onion, finely chopped

Wash the bean sprouts in cold water, discarding the husks and other bits and pieces that float to the surface. It is not necessary to top and tail each sprout. Thinly shred the pepper.

Heat a wok or large pot, add the oil and wait for it to smoke. Add the bean sprouts and red pepper and stir a few times. Add the salt and water. When the soup starts to boil, garnish with finely chopped green onion and serve hot.

PEKING SLICED FISH PEPPER POT SOUP

SERVES 4–6

8oz white fish fillets
1½tsp salt
1tbsp cornstarch
1 egg white
2 slices fresh ginger root
1 clove garlic
2 green onions
vegetable oil for deep-frying
4 cups chicken stock
½tsp salt
¼tsp monosodium glutamate
¼ cup wine vinegar
½tsp pepper

Cut the fish into 1½×1 inch slices. Dust with the 1½ tsp salt and the cornstarch, and wet with the egg white. Finely chop the ginger and garlic. Coarsely chop the green onions.

Heat the oil in a wok or deep-fryer. When hot, lightly fry the coated fish for 1 minute. Remove and drain. Bring the stock to a boil in the wok or saucepan. Add the ginger, garlic,

remaining salt and monosodium glutamate, if using, and bring back to a boil for 1 minute. Add the fish, vinegar and pepper and simmer for 3–4 minutes. Pour into a heated tureen, sprinkle with green onions and serve.

SWEETCORN AND ASPARAGUS SOUP

SERVES 4–6

6oz white asparagus
1 egg white
1tbsp cornstarch
3tbsp water
2½ cups water
1tsp salt
4oz sweetcorn
1 green onion, finely chopped, to garnish

Cut the asparagus spears into small cubes. Beat the egg white lightly. Mix the cornstarch with the water to make a smooth paste. Bring the water to a rolling boil. Add the salt, sweetcorn and asparagus. When the

water starts to boil again, add the cornstarch and water mixture, stirring constantly. Add the egg white very slowly and stir. Serve hot, garnished with finely chopped green onions.

CUCUMBER SOUP

SERVES 4–6

½ cucumber
2oz black field mushrooms
2 cups water
1½tsp salt
1tsp sesame seed oil
1 green onion, finely chopped

Split the cucumber in half lengthwise, and thinly slice but do not peel. Wash and slice the mushrooms, but do not peel. Bring the water to a boil in a wok or large pot. Add the cucumber and mushroom slices and salt. Boil for about 1 minute. Add the sesame seed oil and finely chopped green onion, stir and serve hot.

LEFT: BEAN SPROUT SOUP
RIGHT: CUCUMBER SOUP

FUKIEN CRAB RICE

SERVES 6–8

1 bowl cooked glutinous rice
2 bowls cooked long grain rice
8–12oz young leeks
3 slices fresh ginger root
2 cloves garlic
2 medium crabs, about 3lb
¼pt vegetable oil
2tbsp lard
1tsp salt
¼ cup good stock (see recipe)
1 chicken stock cube
3tbsp tomato paste
1tsp paprika
1tbsp light soy sauce
⅔ cup dry sherry
1tbsp cornstarch blended with 3tbsp water

Place the bowl of glutinous rice in a saucepan with 1½ bowls of water. Bring to a boil and simmer very gently for 15 minutes. Add this rice to the cooked long grain rice and mix together. Clean and cut the leeks slantwise into 2 inch sections. Shred the ginger. Coarsely chop the garlic. Chop each crab through the shell into 12 pieces, cracking the claws with the side of the chopper. Discard the dead men's fingers.

Heat the oil in a wok or large skillet. When very hot, add the crab pieces and turn them around in the hot oil for 3 minutes. Drain. Pour away the oil to use for other purposes, leaving 3 tbsp. Add the lard and reheat the wok or skillet. When hot, stir-fry the ginger and garlic over medium heat for 15 seconds. Add the leeks and salt and stir-fry for 1 minute. Pour in the stock and sprinkle in the crumbled stock cube, then add the tomato paste, paprika, soy sauce and sherry. Bring to a boil, stirring, and return the crab pieces to the pan. Cook over medium heat for 3 minutes. Add the blended cornstarch, turn and stir a few times until thickened.

Place the mixed rice into a medium two-handled wok with a lid, or a large flameproof casserole. Pour the crab and leek mixture over the rice.

Place the wok or casserole over a low heat, cover and cook gently for 5 minutes. Bring the container to the table for serving.

BASIC FRIED RICE

SERVES 4

2 medium onions
2–3 rashers of bacon
2 green onions
3 eggs
6tbsp vegetable oil
¼ cup peas
2 bowls plain boiled rice
1tsp salt

Peel and thinly slice the onions. Cut the bacon across the lean and fat into matchstick-sized strips. Cut the green onions into ¼ inch shreds. Lightly beat the eggs.

Heat 3 tbsp of the oil in a wok or skillet. When hot, stir-fry the onion and bacon over medium heat for 1 minute.

Add the peas and continue to stir-fry for 45 seconds. Add the cooked rice and toss and turn for 45 seconds. Remove from the heat. Heat the remaining oil in a separate small wok or skillet. When hot, add half the green onions and stir over medium heat for 30 seconds. Pour in the beaten egg. Tilt the pan, so that the egg flows evenly over the bottom of the pan. After 1 minute, when the eggs have nearly set, sprinkle with the salt and the remainder of the green onions. Stir and lightly scramble the eggs. When set, transfer the egg mixture to the rice. Stir and turn over medium heat for 1 minute.

YANCHOW FRIED RICE

◆ RICE AND NOODLES ◆

YANCHOW FRIED RICE

SERVES 5–6

1 recipe Basic Fried Rice (see recipe)
1 medium red bell pepper
2–3oz bean sprouts
3oz fresh or frozen medium or large
  prawns
2–3oz canned straw mushrooms or 4oz
  fresh button mushrooms
1 medium zucchini
3tbsp vegetable oil
3tbsp sweetcorn
3oz fresh or frozen shrimps
1tbsp lard or butter
1½tbsp light soy sauce

Repeat the Basic Fried Rice recipe. Cut the red pepper into ¼ inch pieces. Wash and dry the bean sprouts. Cut each shrimp into 2–3 pieces. If using button mushrooms, quarter them. Cut the zucchini into 8 sections, then further divide into quarters.

Heat the oil in a wok or skillet. When hot, stir-fry the pepper, mushrooms, bean sprouts, zucchini, shrimp and prawns over high heat for 1½ minutes. Add the lard and light soy sauce and continue to stir-fry over medium heat for 1½ minutes. Turn the contents into the pan containing the fried rice. Reduce the heat to low, turn and stir together for 30 seconds.

SHANGHAI VEGETABLE RICE

SERVES 5–6

2½ cups long grain rice
1lb green cabbage or spring greens
2tbsp dried shrimps
about 8oz Chinese sausages
3tbsp vegetable oil
1½tbsp lard
1½tsp salt

SHANGHAI VEGETABLE RICE

Wash and measure the rice. Simmer in the same volume of water for 6 minutes. Remove from the heat and leave to stand, covered, for 7–8 minutes. Wash and dry the cabbage. Chop into 1½×3 inch pieces, removing the tougher stalks. Soak the dried shrimps in hot water to cover for 7–8 minutes, then drain. Cut the sausages slantwise into 1 inch sections.

Heat the oil and lard in a deep saucepan. When hot, stir-fry the shrimps for 30 seconds. Add the cabbage and toss and turn for 1½ minutes until well coated with oil. Sprinkle the cabbage with the salt. Pack in the rice. Push pieces of sausage into the rice. Add ½ cup water down the side of the pan. Cover and simmer very gently for about 15 minutes. Transfer to a heated serving dish.

◆ RICE AND NOODLES ◆

VEGETARIAN SPECIAL FRIED RICE

SERVES 4–6

4–6 dried Chinese mushrooms
1 green bell pepper, cored and seeded
1 red bell pepper, cored and seeded
⅔ cup bamboo shoots
2 eggs
2 green onions, finely chopped
2tsp salt
5–6tbsp oil
2lb cooked rice
1tbsp light soy sauce (optional)

Soak the dried mushrooms in warm water for 25–30 minutes, squeeze dry and discard the hard stalks. Cut the mushrooms into small cubes. Cut the green and red peppers and the bamboo shoots into small cubes. Lightly beat the eggs with about half of the green onions and a pinch of the salt.

Heat about 3 tbsp oil in a hot wok, add the beaten eggs and scramble until set. Remove. Heat the remaining oil. When hot, add the rest of the green onions followed by all the vegetables and stir-fry until each piece is covered with oil. Add the cooked rice and salt and stir to separate each grain of rice. Finally add the soy sauce, blend everything together and serve.

SHANGHAI EMERALD FRIED RICE

SERVES 4–6

8oz green greens or cabbage
2tsp salt
6–7tbsp vegetable oil
2 eggs
2 green onions
1lb cooked rice (see recipe)
3tbsp chopped ham
¼tsp monosodium glutamate (optional)

Wash and finely shred the cabbage. Sprinkle with 1½ tsp of the salt. Toss and leave to season for 10 minutes. Squeeze dry. Heat 2 tbsp of the oil in a wok or skillet. When hot, stir-fry the cabbage for 30 seconds. Remove

from the skillet. Add 1 tbsp oil to the wok or skillet. When hot, add the beaten eggs to form a thin pancake. As soon as the egg sets, remove from the pan and chop. Chop the green onions.

Heat 3–4tbsp oil in a wok or skillet. When hot, stir-fry the green onion for a few seconds. Add the rice and stir with the green onion. Reduce the heat to low, stir and turn until the rice is heated through. Add the cabbage, egg and ham. Stir and mix them together well. Sprinkle with monosodium glutamate, if using, and remaining salt. Stir and turn once more, then sprinkle with remaining egg.

PLAIN COOKED RICE GRUEL OR CONGEE

SERVES 4–6

2 cups or bowls long grain white rice
5 pints or bowls water

Wash and rinse the rice, drain well. Place in a deep heavy pot or pan and add the water. Bring to a boil, reduce the heat and simmer very gently, uncovered, for 1½ hours, stirring occasionally. By this time, the rice will be fairly thick and porridgy; suitable for serving for breakfast or late supper. Serve accompanied by pickled or salted foods.

VEGETARIAN NOODLES IN SOUP

SERVES 4–6

8oz water chestnuts
4oz straw mushrooms
4oz white nuts
¼ cup oil
1tsp salt
1tsp sugar
1tbsp light soy sauce
1tsp sesame seed oil
8oz egg noodles or vermicelli

Drain the ingredients if they are canned and cut the water chestnuts into thin slices. The straw mush-

rooms and white nuts can be left whole.

Heat the oil in a wok or skillet. When it starts to smoke, add the vegetables and stir-fry for a few seconds. Add the salt, sugar and soy sauce and continue stirring. When the gravy begins to boil, reduce the heat and let it simmer gently.

Cook the noodles in boiling water. Drain and place them in a large serving bowl. Pour a little of the water in which the noodles were cooked into the bowl – just enough to half-cover the noodles. Then quickly pour the entire contents of the wok or skillet over the top. Garnish with the sesame seed oil and serve hot.

BEGGARS' NOODLES

SERVES 6

Good
Quite rich

3 green onions
¼ cup soy sauce
¼ cup wine vinegar
1lb wheat flour noodles, flat or Ho Fen noodles, or spaghetti

Sauce
¼ cup peanut butter
3tbsp sesame paste
¼ cup sesame seed oil

Coarsely chop or shred the onions. Mix the soy sauce and vinegar together. Mix the peanut butter, sesame paste and sesame seed oil together.

Place the noodles in a saucepan of boiling water and simmer for 10 minutes, or spaghetti for about 10–12 minutes. Drain.

Divide the hot noodles into 4–6 heated large rice bowls. Sprinkle evenly with the green onion. Add a large spoonful of the peanut butter and sesame mixture to each bowl of noodles. Pour 1 tbsp of soy sauce and vinegar mixture over contents of each bowl.

OPPOSITE: BEGGARS' NOODLES

◆ RICE AND NOODLES ◆

◆ VEGETABLES, BEAN CURD AND EGG ◆

SHANGHAI SPRING ROLLS

SERVES 12

6 dried Chinese mushrooms, soaked in warm water for 30 minutes
2 cakes fresh tofu
8oz finely ground pork
peanut or corn oil for frying
8oz cooked shrimp, chopped coarsely
½tsp cornstarch, mixed to a paste with 1tbsp light soy sauce
½ cup each bamboo shoots and water chestnuts, sliced finely
1½ cups bean sprouts
6 green onions, finely chopped
a little sesame seed oil
12 spring roll wrappers, thawed and separated, covered with damp cloth
deep fat for frying
hoisin sauce for dipping

Drain the mushrooms, remove stalks and cut into fine matchstick-like pieces; slice the tofu similarly. Fry the ground pork in a little hot oil until it changes color, stirring all the time. Cook for 2–3 minutes. Add the shrimp, then the cornstarch paste and keep breaking up the mixture with a slice. Now add the bamboo shoots, water chestnuts, bean sprouts and green onions over high heat, stirring all the time. Add the mushrooms and tofu. Taste for seasoning and stir in the sesame seed oil away from the heat. Allow to cool before filling the spring roll wrappers. Deep-fry in the same way and drain them one by one on paper. Serve hot with hoisin sauce for dipping.

PICKLED VEGETABLES

Use four to six of the following vegetables, or more:

cucumber
carrot
radish or turnip
cauliflower
broccoli
green cabbage
white cabbage
celery
onion
fresh ginger root
leek
green onion
red bell pepper
green bell pepper
string beans
garlic
1 gallon boiled water, cooled
¾ cup salt
2oz chili peppers
3tsp Sichuan peppercorns
¼ cup Chinese distilled spirit (or white rum, gin or vodka)
4oz fresh ginger root
½ cup brown sugar

Put the cold boiled water into a large, clean earthenware or glass jar. Add the salt, chilies, peppercorns, spirit, ginger and sugar.

Wash and trim the vegetables, peel if necessary and drain well. Put them into the jar and seal it, making sure it is airtight. Place the jar in a cool place and leave the vegetables to pickle for at least five days before serving.

Use a pair of clean chopsticks or tongs to pick the vegetables out of the jar. Do not allow any grease to enter the jar. You can replenish the vegetables, adding a little salt each time. If any white scum appears on the surface of the brine, add a little sugar and spirit. The longer the pickling lasts, the better.

VEGETARIAN "LION'S HEAD" CASSEROLE

SERVES 4–6

4 cakes fresh tofu
4oz fried gluten
2oz cooked carrots
4–5 dried Chinese mushrooms, soaked
⅓ cup bamboo shoots
6 cabbage or lettuce hearts
5 large cabbage leaves
1tsp fresh ginger root, finely chopped
3tbsp rice wine or dry sherry
1tbsp salt
1tsp sugar
1tsp white pepper (ground)
2tsp sesame seed oil
1tbsp cornstarch

◆ VEGETABLES, BEAN CURD AND EGG ◆

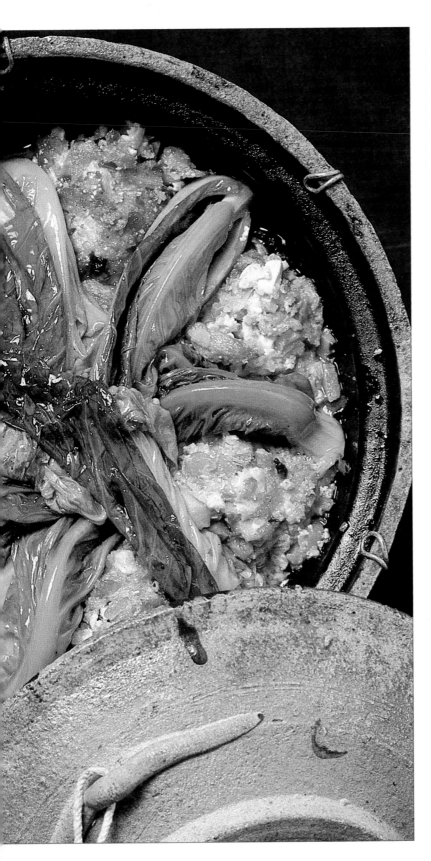

1oz ground rice or bread crumbs
oil for deep-frying
All-purpose flour for dusting

Squeeze as much liquid as possible from the tofu using cheese cloth or muslin and then mash. Finely chop the gluten, carrots, mushrooms and bamboo shoots. Place them with the mashed tofu in a large mixing bowl. Add 1 tsp salt, the finely chopped ginger root, ground rice, cornstarch and sesame seed oil and blend everything together until smooth. Make 10 "meatballs" from this mixture and place them on a plate lightly dusted with flour. Trim off any hard or tough roots from the cabbage or lettuce hearts.

Heat the oil in a wok or deep-fryer. When hot, deep-fry the "meatballs" for about 3 minutes, stirring very gently to make sure that they are not stuck together. Scoop out with a slotted spoon or strainer and drain.

Pour off the excess oil leaving about 3 tbsp in the wok. Stir-fry the cabbage hearts with a little salt and sugar. Add about 2½ cups water and bring to a boil. Reduce the heat and let the mixture simmer.

Meanwhile, line the bottom of a casserole with the cabbage leaves and place the "meatballs" on top. Pour the cabbage hearts with the soup in the casserole and add the remaining salt, ground pepper and wine or sherry. Cover, bring to a boil, reduce the heat and simmer for 10 minutes.

To serve, take off the lid and re-arrange the cabbage hearts so that they appear between the "meatballs" in a star-shaped pattern.

VEGETARIAN "LION'S HEAD" CASSEROLE

◆ VEGETABLES, BEAN CURD AND EGG ◆

HOT AND SOUR CUCUMBER — SICHUAN STYLE

SERVES 4–6

1 cucumber
1tsp salt
3tbsp sugar
3tbsp vinegar
1tbsp chili oil

Split the cucumber in two length-wise and then cut each piece into strips rather like potato chips. Sprinkle with the salt and leave for about 10 minutes to extract the bitter juices.

Remove each cucumber strip. Place it on a firm surface and soften it by gently tapping it with the blade of a cleaver or knife.

Place the cucumber strips on a plate. Sprinkle the sugar evenly over them and then add the vinegar and chili oil just before serving.

VEGETARIAN SPRING ROLLS

1 pack of 20 frozen spring roll skins
8oz fresh bean sprouts
8oz young tender leeks or green onions
4oz carrots
4oz white mushrooms
oil for deep-frying
1½tsp salt
1tsp sugar
1tbsp light soy sauce

Take the spring roll skins out of the packet and leave them to defrost thoroughly under a damp cloth. Wash and rinse the bean sprouts in a bowl of cold water and discard the husks and other bits and pieces that float to the surface. Drain. Cut the leeks or green onions, carrots and mushrooms into thin shreds.

To cook the filling, heat 3–4 tbsp of oil in a preheated wok or skillet and stir-fry all the vegetables for a few seconds. Add the salt, sugar and soy sauce and continue stirring for about 1–1½ minutes. Remove and leave to cool a little.

To cook the spring rolls, heat about 6¼ cups oil in a wok or deep-fryer until it smokes. Reduce the heat or even turn it off for a few minutes to cool the oil a little before adding the spring rolls. Deep-fry 6–8 at a time for 3–4 minutes or until golden and crispy. Increase the heat to high again before frying each batch. As each batch is cooked, remove and drain it on paper towels. Serve hot with a dip sauce such as soy sauce, vinegar, chili sauce or mustard.

These spring rolls are ideal for a buffet-style meal or as cocktail snacks.

HOT AND SOUR CUCUMBER — SICHUAN STYLE

◆ VEGETABLES, BEAN CURD AND EGG ◆

SAN SHIAN — "THE THREE DELICACIES"

SERVES 4–6

9oz winter bamboo shoots
4oz oyster or straw mushrooms
10oz fried gluten or deep-fried tofu
4tbsp oil
1½tsp salt
1tsp sugar
1tbsp light soy sauce
1tsp sesame seed oil
fresh cilantro leaves to garnish (optional)

Cut the bamboo shoots into thin slices. The oyster mushrooms can be left whole if small; otherwise halve or quarter them. Straw mushrooms can be left whole.

Heat the oil in a hot wok or skillet, swirling it so that most of the surface is well greased. When the oil starts to smoke, add the bamboo shoots and mushrooms and stir-fry for about 1 minute. Add the gluten or tofu together with salt, sugar and soy

sauce. Continue stirring for 1–1½ minutes longer, adding a little water if necessary. Finally add the sesame seed oil, blend well and serve hot.

This dish can also be served cold. In that case, you might like to separate the three main ingredients, arrange them in three neat rows and garnish with fresh cilantro.

QUICK-FRIED GREEN BEANS WITH DRIED SHRIMPS AND PORK

SERVES 4–6

1½lb green beans
3tbsp dried shrimps
1tbsp chopped Sichuan Ja Chai hot pickle
vegetable oil for deep-frying
1½tbsp lard
3tsp garlic, chopped
3oz ground pork
¼ cup good stock (see recipe)
1tbsp soy sauce
½tbsp sugar
2tsp salt

VEGETARIAN SPRING ROLLS

¼ cup water
1tsp sesame seed oil
2tsp vinegar
3tbsp chopped green onions (optional)

Trim the green beans. Soak the dried shrimp in hot water to cover for 20 minutes. Drain and chop. Finely chop the pickle.

Heat the oil in a wok or deep-fryer. When hot, fry the beans for 2 minutes. Remove and put aside. Pour away the oil to use for other purposes. Heat the lard in the wok or skillet. When hot, add the garlic and stir a few times. Add the pork, shrimps, stock and pickle and stir-fry for 2 minutes. Stir in the soy sauce, sugar, salt and water. Add the green beans and turn and toss until the liquid in the pan has nearly all evaporated. Sprinkle with the sesame seed oil, vinegar and green onions. Turn and stir once more, then serve.

◆ VEGETABLES, BEAN CURD AND EGG ◆

STIR-FRIED BEAN SPROUTS WITH GREEN PEPPERS

SERVES 4–6

1lb fresh bean sprouts
1 small green bell pepper, cored and seeded
1–2 green onions
¼ cup oil
1tsp salt
1tsp sugar

Wash and rinse the bean sprouts in cold water, discarding the husks and other bits and pieces that float to the surface. Cut the green pepper into thin shreds. Cut the green onions into short lengths.

Heat the oil in a hot wok until smoking. Add the green onions and green pepper, stir a few times, and then add the bean sprouts. Continue stirring.

After about 30 seconds, add salt and sugar, and stir a few times more. do not overcook because the sprouts will become soggy. This dish can be served either hot or cold.

STIR-FRIED SPINACH AND TOFU

SERVES 4–6

8oz spinach
2 cakes fresh tofu
⅓ cup oil
1tsp salt
1tsp sugar
1tbsp soy sauce
1tsp sesame seed oil

Wash the spinach well, shaking off the excess water. Cup up each cake of tofu into about 8 pieces.

Heat the oil in a wok. Fry the tofu pieces until they are golden, turning them over once or twice gently. Remove them with a slotted spoon and set aside.

Stir-fry the spinach in the remaining oil for about 30 seconds or until the leaves are limp. Add the tofu pieces, salt, sugar and soy sauce, blend well and cook for another 1–1½ minutes. Add the sesame seed oil and serve hot.

EGGPLANT WITH SICHUAN "FISH SAUCE"

SERVES 4–6

1lb eggplant
4–5 dried red chili peppers
oil for deep-frying
3–4 green onions, finely chopped
1 slice fresh ginger root, peeled and finely chopped
1 clove garlic, finely chopped
1tsp sugar
1tbsp soy sauce
1tbsp vinegar
1tbsp chili bean paste
2tsp cornstarch, mixed with 3tbsp water
1tsp sesame seed oil

Soak the dried red chilies for 5-10 minutes, cut them into small pieces and discard the stalks. Peel the eggplants, discard the stalks and cut them into diamond-shaped chunks.

Heat the oil in a wok and deep-fry the eggplants for 3½–4 minutes or until soft. Remove with a slotted spoon and drain.

ABOVE: CHINESE CABBAGE WITH CHILIES
RIGHT: FU YUNG CAULIFLOWER

Pour off the oil and return the eggplants to the wok with the red chilies, green onions, ginger root and garlic. Stir a few times and add the sugar, soy sauce, vinegar and chili bean paste. Stir for 1 minute. Add cornstarch and water mixture, blend well and garnish with sesame seed oil. Serve hot or cold.

FU-YUNG CAULIFLOWER

SERVES 4–6

1 large cauliflower
2 egg whites
4oz finely chopped breast of chicken
⅓ cup good stock (see recipe)
1½tbsp cornstarch blended with ⅓ cup water
salt and pepper to taste
⅓ cup milk

Remove the cauliflower stalk. Cut the cauliflower into flowerets. Beat the

◆ VEGETABLES, BEAN CURD AND EGG ◆

egg whites until nearly stiff. Mix in all the remaining ingredients thoroughly. Lightly beat together.

Place the cauliflower flowerets in a saucepan of boiling water and simmer for 7–8 minutes. Drain. Put the cauliflower in a wok or pan. Add the egg white and chicken mixture. bring to a boil, reduce the heat and gently simmer for 3 minutes, stirring and turning gently.

Transfer the cauliflower to a heated dish and pour the sauce over. If liked, sprinkle with chopped green onion

and finely chopped ham or pre-soaked, chopped dried shrimps.

CHINESE WHITE CABBAGE WITH CHILIES

SERVES 5–6

1 Chinese white cabbage, about 3½lb
3 small fresh red chilies
2 dried red chilies
1½tsp Sichuan peppercorns

2tsp salt
½tsp sesame seed oil
1tbsp vegetable oil

Chop the cabbage coarsely, discarding the tougher parts. Coarsely chop the chilies, discarding the seeds. Pound the peppercorns lightly. Place the cabbage in a large bowl, sprinkle evenly with the salt, chilies and peppercorns. Toss to mix. Refrigerate for 2–3 days before serving. Sprinkle the cabbage with the oils; toss well and serve.

◆ VEGETABLES, BEAN CURD AND EGG ◆

STEWED GLUTEN IN SWEET BEAN SAUCE

SERVES 4–6

See the recipe for Fried Gluten

11oz gluten in small pieces
¼ cup oil
1tbsp dark soy sauce
1tbsp sugar
1tsp five-spice powder
3tbsp rice wine or dry sherry
1tbsp sweet bean paste
1 slice fresh ginger root, crushed
2tsp sesame seed oil

Boil the gluten pieces in a pan of water for about 4–5 minutes or until they float to the surface. Remove and drain off as much water as possible.

Heat the oil in a hot wok or pan. When hot, add the boiled gluten, stir for a few seconds and then add the soy sauce, sugar, five-spice powder, wine, sweet bean paste, crushed ginger root and about ½ cup water.

Bring to a boil and cook over high heat for 20–25 minutes or until there is very little juice left, stirring now and again to make sure that each piece of gluten is well covered by the gravy.

Add the sesame seed oil, blend well and serve hot or cold.

FRIED GLUTEN

SERVES 4–6

2lb flour
1tbsp salt
18–19fl oz warm water
oil for deep-frying
1tsp salt
1tsp sugar
1tbsp light soy sauce
¼tsp monosodium glutamate (optional)

Sift the flour into a large mixing bowl. Add the salt and the water gradually to make a firm dough. Knead until smooth and then cover with a damp cloth and leave to stand for about 1 hour.

Place the dough in a large colander

FRIED GLUTEN

or strainer and run cold water over it while you press and squeeze the dough with your hands to wash out as much of the starch as you can. After 10–15 minutes of this hard work, you will end up with about 11oz gluten. Squeeze off as much water as you can and then cut the gluten into about 35–40 small pieces. These can be cooked either by deep-frying or boiling (or they can be steamed or baked).

Heat the oil in a wok or deep-fryer. When hot, deep-fry the gluten in batches – about 6 to 8 at a time – for about 3 minutes or until they turn golden. Remove and drain.

Pour off the excess oil, leaving about 1 tbsp in the wok. Return the partly cooked gluten to the wok, add salt, sugar and soy sauce (and the monosodium glutamate if used), stir, and add a little water if necessary. Braise for about 2 minutes. Serve hot or cold.

◆ FISH AND CRUSTACEANS ◆

FRIED BASS IN SWEET AND SOUR SAUCE

SERVES 2–4

1 sea bass weighing about 1½–2lb
1tsp salt
3tbsp flour
oil for deep-frying

Sauce
3tbsp sugar
3tbsp vinegar
1tbsp soy sauce
½tbsp cornstarch
3tbsp stock or water

Garnish
2 green onions
2 slices fresh ginger root, peeled
1 small red bell pepper
fresh cilantro

Clean and scale the fish, slash both sides diagonally at intervals. Rub salt both inside and out, then coat with flour.

Thinly shred the onions, ginger root and red pepper.

Deep-fry the fish in hot oil until golden; place it on a long dish.

Pour off the excess oil from the wok, put in the sauce mixture and stir until smooth, then pour it over the fish. Garnish with shredded onions, ginger root, red pepper and cilantro.

FISH-HEAD CASSEROLE

SERVES 4–6

1 fish-head weighing about 1lb
2oz lean pork
3–4 dried Chinese mushrooms, soaked
2 cakes fresh tofu
2 slices fresh ginger root
2 green onions
1tsp salt
3tbsp rice wine or dry sherry
1tbsp sugar
3tbsp soy sauce

3tbsp flour
1¼ cup stock
oil for deep-drying

Garnish
green onions
red chili
fresh cilantro

Discard the gills from the fish-head; rub some salt both inside and out; coat the head with flour.

Cut the pork, mushrooms, tofu and ginger root into small slices; cut the onions into short lengths.

Deep-fry the fish-head over a moderate heat for 10 minutes or until golden. Remove.

Heat a little oil in a sand-pot or casserole. Put in the ginger root and onions, followed by pork, mushrooms and stir for a while, then add rice wine or sherry, sugar, soy sauce, stock and the fish-head; bring it to a boil; add a little salt; reduce heat; simmer for 7 minutes.

Garnish with onions, red chili and fresh cilantro. Serve in a sand-pot or casserole.

ABOVE RIGHT: FRIED BASS IN SWEET AND SOUR SAUCE
RIGHT: FISH-HEAD CASSEROLE

◆ FISH AND CRUSTACEANS ◆

STEAMED WHOLE FISH WRAPPED IN LOTUS LEAVES

SERVES 4–6

1 whole fish, about 2lb
2tbsp dark soy sauce
2 lotus leaves
¼ cup vegetable oil

Garnish and sauce
3–4oz canned snow pickles
3 slices fresh ginger root
2 green onions
2 fresh chilies
3tbsp light soy sauce
3tbsp rice wine or dry sherry
½ cup good stock
2tsp sugar

Clean the fish and dry well. Rub inside and out with the soy sauce. Shred the pickles, ginger, green onions and fresh chilies, discarding seeds. Soak the lotus leaves in warm water for 10 minutes to soften. Drain.

Heat the oil in a wok or skillet. When hot, stir-fry pickles, green onions, ginger and chilies over medium heat for 1 minute. Add the soy sauce, rice wine or sherry, stock and sugar, bring to a boil and stir for 30 seconds. Place the fish on the lotus leaves. Pour half the contents of the wok or pan over the length of the fish. Turn the fish over and pour over the remainder. Wrap the fish completely in the lotus leaves. Secure by tying with string. Place in a steamer and steam for 25 minutes.

SQUIRREL FISH

SERVES 4–6

1 whole fish, 1½–2lb
3 slices fresh ginger root
1½tsp salt
pepper to taste
¼–⅓ cup cornstarch
vegetable oil for deep-frying

Sauce
3tbsp wood ears (tree fungus)
6 medium dried Chinese mushrooms

◆ FISH AND CRUSTACEANS ◆

2 green onions
2 tbsp lard
3 tbsp drained, canned bamboo shoots
¼ cup soy sauce
1 tbsp sugar
⅓ cup good stock (see recipe)
3 tbsp wine vinegar
3 tbsp rice wine or dry sherry

This dish derives its name from the fact that, when cooked and served, the fish's tail curves up like a squirrel's.

Clean the fish and slit open from head to tail on the underside so that it lays flat. Cut 7–8 deep slashes on one side of the fish and only 2 on the other side. Finely chop the ginger. Rub the fish inside and out with the salt, pepper and ginger, then coat in the cornstarch. Soak the wood ears and mushrooms separately in hot water to cover for 25 minutes. Drain and discard the tough stalks. Cut the mushroom caps into shreds. Finely slice the wood ears. Cut the green onions into 2 inch sections.

Heat the oil in a wok or deep-fryer. When hot, gently fry the fish over medium heat for 4 minutes, then reduce the heat to low. Meanwhile, melt the lard in a smaller wok or pan. When hot, stir-fry the wood ears, mushrooms, green onions and bamboo shoots over medium heat for 1½ minutes. Add the soy sauce, sugar, stock, vinegar and wine or sherry. Stir the ingredients over low heat for about 2 minutes. Raise the heat under the wok containing the fish and fry for another 2 minutes. The tail should have curled by now due to the uneven amount of cuts on the fish. Lift out the fish, drain and place on a heated dish.

STEAMED WHOLE FISH WRAPPED IN LOTUS LEAVES

◆ FISH AND CRUSTACEANS ◆

STEAMED FISH WITH GARNISH

SERVES 4–5

1 whole fish, about 1½–2lb
2tsp salt
pepper to taste
1½tbsp fresh ginger root, finely chopped

Garnish and sauce
2–3 green onions
3 slices fresh ginger root
3 large fresh or dried Chinese mushrooms
   (optional)
1tbsp rice wine or dry sherry
3tbsp soy sauce
⅓ cup vegetable oil

Clean the fish and dry well. Rub inside and out with the salt, pepper and finely chopped ginger. Leave to season for 30 minutes. Shred the green onions and ginger. Slice the mushroom caps; if using dried, soak first in hot water for 25 minutes.

Place the fish on a heatproof dish and put into a steamer. Steam vigorously for 10 minutes. Remove the dish from the steamer and pour away any excess water which has collected. Pour the rice wine or sherry and soy sauce down the length of the fish and garnish the fish with the green onions, mushrooms and ginger. Heat the oil in a small pan and, when smoking hot, pour it in a thin stream down the length of the fish over the green onions, mushrooms and ginger. The fish is brought to the table on the dish in which it was cooked.

SAUTÉED FISH STEAKS WITH GARNISH

SERVES 4–6

1½–2lb fish, cut into 4–6 steaks
2tsp salt
pepper to taste
½ cup vegetable oil
5 slices fresh ginger root

Garnish and sauce
4 medium dried Chinese mushrooms

2 green onions
1¼oz lard
3tbsp onion, coarsely chopped
1½tbsp fresh ginger root, chopped
4oz ground pork
¼ cup soy sauce
⅓ cup good stock
3tbsp rice wine or dry sherry

Clean and dry the fish steaks. Rub with the salt, pepper and 1 tbsp of the oil. Soak the dried mushrooms in hot water to cover for 25 minutes. Drain and discard the tough stalks. Cut the mushroom caps into match–stick-sized shreds. Cut the green onions into 1 inch sections.

Heat the remaining oil in a wok or skillet. When hot, add the ginger slices and spread out evenly to flavor the oil. Lay the fish steaks in the hot flavored oil and shallow-fry or sauté for 2 minutes on each side. Pour away any excess oil and remove from the heat. Heat the lard in a separate pan. When hot, stir-fry the chopped onion, ginger and mushrooms for 1 minute. Add the ground pork and stir over high heat for 3 minutes. Mix in the soy sauce stock, wine or sherry and green onion. Bring to a boil and continue to stir-fry for 1 minute. Meanwhile, reheat the first pan and return the fish steaks to it. Heat through, then pour the sauce and garnish over the fish. Transfer contents to a heated serving plate.

BRAISED WHOLE FISH IN HOT VINEGAR SAUCE

SERVES 4–6

2 slices fresh ginger root
1 whole fish, 1½–2lb
1tsp salt
pepper to taste
⅓ cup vegetable oil

Sauce
3 slices fresh ginger root
⅓ cup canned bamboo shoots, drained
½ red pepper
1 small carrot
1 green chili
2 dried chilies

2 green onions
2tbsp lard
3tbsp light soy sauce
¼ cup good stock
½ cup vinegar
½tbsp cornstarch blended with 3tbsp
   water

Finely chop the 2 slices of ginger. Clean the fish and dry well. Rub evenly inside and out with salt, pepper, chopped ginger and 1 tbsp of the oil. Leave to season for 30 minutes. Shred the 3 slices of ginger, bamboo shoots, red pepper, carrot, chilies, discarding seeds, and green onions.

Heat the remaining oil in a wok or skillet. When hot, fry the fish for 2½ minutes on each side. Remove and drain. Add the shredded ginger, bamboo shoots, red pepper, carrot, chilies and green onions to the remaining oil and stir-fry over medium heat for 1 minute. Add the lard, soy sauce, stock and half the vinegar and cook for another minute. Lay the fish back in the wok or pan and cook gently for 2 minutes on both sides, basting. Transfer the fish to a serving dish. Stir the remaining vinegar into the wok, then add the blended cornstarch, stirring over high heat until the sauce thickens.

Pour the sauce from the wok over the length of the fish and garnish with the shredded vegetables.

BEAN CURD FISH IN CHILI SAUCE

SERVES 2–3

1lb mullet or mackerel
2 green onions, white parts only
1 clove garlic
2 slices fresh ginger root
2 cakes fresh tofu
1tsp salt
⅓ cup oil
3tbsp chili paste
1tbsp soy sauce
3tbsp rice wine or dry sherry
3tbsp cornstarch
12fl oz (350ml) stock

◆ FISH AND CRUSTACEANS ◆

Cut the heads off the fish and remove the backbone; crush the garlic, cut it and the ginger root into small pieces; cut the onion whites into short lengths.

Cut each tofu cube into about 10 pieces. Blanch them in boiling water; remove and soak them in stock with salt.

Heat up the oil until hot; fry the fish until both sides are golden; put them to one side; tilt the wok, and put in the chili paste. When it starts to bubble, return the wok to its original position, push the fish back, add soy sauce, wine or sherry, onion, ginger root, garlic and a little stock — about ½ cup. At the same time add the tofu taken from the stock and cook with the fish for about 10 minutes.

Now pick out the fish with chopsticks and place them on a serving dish, then quickly mix the cornstarch with a little cold water. Add to the wok to make a smooth sauce with the tofu; pour it all over the fish and serve.

CHRYSANTHEMUM FISH POT

SERVES 4–6

4oz fish maw
4oz chicken breast meat, boned and skinned
2 chicken gizzards
½lb pig's tripe
4oz Béche-de-Mer
4oz snow peas
½lb spinach leaves
2oz fresh cilantro
2 slices fresh ginger root, peeled
2–3 green onions
2tsp salt
1tsp Sichuan pepper, freshly ground
4½ pints stock (see recipe)

BRAISED WHOLE FISH IN HOT VINEGAR SAUCE

1 large dry chrysanthemum (white or yellow)

Cut the fish maw, chicken gizzards, Béche-de-Mer and tripe into slices. Wash the cabbage, snow peas, spinach and cilantro; cut them into small pieces.

Finely chop the root ginger and onions; place them with salt and pepper in a small bowl.

Bring the stock to a rolling boil in the fire-pot; arrange the meat and vegetables in the moat. They will only need to be cooked for about 5 minutes. Everybody just helps themselves from the pot with chopsticks, and dips their helping in the "four seasonings" before eating it.

Use the chrysanthemum as a decoration.

◆ FISH AND CRUSTACEANS ◆

SWEET-SOUR CRISP FISH

SERVES 2–3

1 carp (or freshwater fish) weighing 1½lb
3tbsp rice wine or dry sherry
⅓ cup soy sauce
2oz cornstarch
1 clove garlic
2 green onions
2 slices fresh ginger root
2 dried red chilies, soaked
2tbsp bamboo shoots
2–3 dried Chinese mushrooms, soaked oil
    for deep-frying
2tbsp sugar
2tbsp vinegar
½ cup stock

Clean the fish; make 6 or 7 diagonal cuts as deep as the bone on each side of the fish. Marinate in rice wine or sherry and 2 tbsp of soy sauce for 5 minutes; remove and wipe dry. Make a paste with 1½ oz cornstarch and water and coat the entire fish evenly.

Finely chop the garlic, 1 onion and slice ginger root. Cut the other onion and ginger root into thin shreds. Cut the soaked red chilies (discarding the seeds), bamboo shoots and mushrooms all into thin shreds.

Heat up the oil to boiling point, pick up the fish by the tail, lower it head first into the oil, turn it around and deep-fry for about 7 minutes or until golden; remove and drain.

Pour off the excess oil leaving about 3 tbsp in the wok; add finely chopped onion, ginger root, garlic and red chili, bamboo shoots and mushrooms followed by the remaining soy sauce, sugar, vinegar and stock. Stir a few times, then add the remaining cornstarch mixed with a little water; blend well to make a slightly thick smooth paste.

Place a cloth over the fish, press gently with your hand to soften the body, then put it on a serving dish and pour the sauce over it; garnish with onion and ginger root shreds.

CRAB BALLS

STEAMED LOBSTER

SERVES 2–4

1 lobster weighing about 1½–2lb

Sauce
2 green onions, finely chopped
2 slices fresh ginger root, finely chopped
1tsp salt
1tsp sugar
½tbsp cornstarch
1tsp sesame seed oil
⅓ cup stock
freshly ground Sichuan pepper
1tbsp oil

Steam the lobster for 20 minutes. Leave to cool, then split in two lengthwise, and cut each half into four pieces.

Crack the shell of the claws so that the flesh can be taken out easily.

Make the sauce by heating up the oil in a wok or saucepan; toss in the finely chopped onions and ginger

root, add salt, sugar, stock and ground pepper. Thicken with the cornstarch mixed with a little water. Finally add the sesame seed oil; pour it all over the lobster and serve.

CRAB BALLS

SERVES 6–8

½lb crab meat
2oz pork fat
½ cup water chestnuts, peeled
2 eggs
3tbsp rice wine or dry sherry
1tsp monosodium glutamate
1tsp salt
3tbsp cornstarch
1 slice fresh ginger root, finely chopped
1 green onion, finely chopped
½ cup chicken stock
1lb lard for deep-frying
1oz cooked ham

Finely chop the crab meat, pork fat and water chestnuts and add 2 eggs,

◆ FISH AND CRUSTACEANS ◆

1 tbsp of wine or sherry, ½ tsp of monosodium glutamate, ½ tsp of salt, and 1 tbsp of cornstarch together with the finely chopped ginger root and onion. Blend well, then make into small balls about the size of walnuts.

Heat up the lard over high heat for about 3–4 minutes, then reduce the heat to moderate and deep-fry the crab balls for about 5 minutes until pale golden. Scoop them out with a perforated spoon and serve them hot or cold. Alternatively place them in a bowl with a little chicken stock — not quite enough to cover them — then place the bowl in a steamer and steam for 15 minutes.

Now mix the remaining wine or sherry, monosodium glutamate, salt and cornstarch with the chicken stock and make a white sauce over a moderate heat, then pour it over the crab balls. Garnish with finely chopped ham and serve.

CRAB WITH EGGS

SERVES 4

4 eggs, beaten
4–6oz crab meat
1tsp sugar
1 small piece fresh ginger root, scraped
*   and crushed in garlic press*
2tsp light soy sauce
seasoning
a little oil for frying
4–6 green onions, finely chopped

Set the beaten egg on one side, pick over the crab meat to remove any shell or cartilage. Stir in sugar, ginger and soy sauce and season to taste. Add this to the beaten eggs and scramble in fat in a pan for 1 minute. Add spring onions and serve at once.

DEEP-FRIED CONPOY AND SHREDDED KALE

SERVES 4–6

3½oz conpoy (dried scallops)
2 slices fresh ginger root

DEEP-FRIED CONPOY AND SHREDDED KALE

1tsp Chinese yellow wine
5oz Chinese kale leaves, or pickled snow
*   cabbage leaves*
2 cups peanut oil
2tsp sugar
1tsp salt

Soak the conpoy in water for 30 minutes. Add the ginger and Chinese yellow wine and steam for 15 minutes. Remove the conpoy, tear it into fine shreds and pat dry. Set it aside.

Cut the Chinese kale leaves into fine shreds, pat it dry and set aside. (If you are using pickled snow cabbage, soak it in 4¼ cups hot water for 30 minutes. Change the water and soak for 30 minutes. Squeeze it dry, tear the leaves into small pieces and set them aside.)

Heat the peanut oil in a pan. Add the conpoy, stirring to separate, and fry until nicely golden in color. Remove, dry and set aside.

Add the kale or cabbage, again stirring to separate, and fry for 1 minute. Remove. If the vegetable is not crispy enough return it to pan for a short time. Remove and pat dry with absorbent paper towels.

Sprinkle 2 tsp of sugar and 1 tsp of salt over the vegetables and mix well. (If you are using pickled snow cabbage, there is no need to add salt.) Place the crispy vegetables on a plate, arrange the conpoy on top and serve.

WINE-MARINATED SHRIMPS

SERVES 4–6

½lb fresh shrimps
¼ cup rice wine or dry sherry
2 green onions, white parts only
2oz celery
2oz carrots
1tbsp peas

Sauce
3tbsp soy sauce
1tsp sesame seed oil

Wash the shrimps well, and place in a dish. Pour the wine or sherry over them, add the onion whites cut to 1 inch lengths; cover and marinate for 5 minutes.

Slice the celery and carrot; parboil with the peas for 5 minutes. Drain and add to the shrimps. Pour the sauce over and serve. Mix the sauce; pour it over the shrimps, serve.

◆ FISH AND CRUSTACEANS ◆

FRIED SHRIMP BALLS WITH BABY CORNS

SERVES 4–6

½lb Pacific prawns
1 small can of baby corns
3–4 dried Chinese mushrooms, soaked
1 slice fresh ginger root
2 green onions
½tbsp salt
1 egg white
1tbsp cornstarch
1tbsp rice wine or dry sherry
1tsp sugar
1tsp sesame seed oil
oil for deep-frying
fresh coriander to garnish

Shell the shrimp; use a sharp knife to make a deep incision down the back of each one, and pull out the black intestinal vein. Cut each shrimp into two or three pieces. Mix with a little salt, egg white and cornstarch.

Finely chop the ginger root and onions, cut large mushrooms into 2 or 3 pieces; smaller ones can be left whole. Drain the baby corns. Deep-fry the prawns in warm oil for 30 seconds; remove and drain.

Pour off the excess oil, leaving about 3 tbsp of oil in the wok, wait until it smokes, toss in the finely chopped ginger root and onions followed by mushrooms, baby corns and prawns; add salt, rice wine or sherry and sugar. Stir until well blended; add sesame seed oil just before serving. Garnish with fresh coriander.

STEAMED EEL

SERVES 4–6

2lb white eel
6 slices fresh ginger root
2 green onions
⅔ cup peanut oil
1tsp Chinese yellow wine
1¼ cups chicken stock
1tsp salt
1tsp sugar
½tsp pepper
1tbsp cornstarch

Put the eel in a basin and pour over it 10 cups boiling water with 3 tbsp of salt added. Wash the fish thoroughly. Slit the eel open, remove the intestines and clean the inside carefully. Pat it dry with absorbent paper towels.

Make deep cuts (about three-quarters of the way through the flesh) at 1 inch intervals along the eel and place it on a plate, bending it into a ring form. Arrange the ginger and green onion on top.

Steam the eel over medium heat for 20 minutes. Remove the ginger and green onions and discard them and drain away the liquid from the plate. Heat the oil and pour it over the eel, again draining any excess from the plate.

Add the remaining ingredients to the pan, stir and bring to a boil. Pour the sauce over the eel and serve.

STEAMED EEL

◆ FISH AND CRUSTACEANS ◆

FRIED OYSTER

SERVES 4–6

12 large oysters
3tbsp cornstarch (for cleaning oysters)
3tbsp salt (for cleaning oysters)
1tsp monosodium glutamate (optional)
1tsp salt

Sauce
⅓ cup wheat flour
3tbsp cornstarch
¾oz powdered yeast
1tsp oil

¼ cup water
2 cups peanut oil (for frying oysters)

Dips
1 small plate of catsup
1 small plate of spiced salt

Rub the oysters thoroughly with cornstarch and salt and then wash them in water. Drop the oysters into a pan of boiling water until they are half cooked (this takes about 20 seconds). Dry the oysters carefully with a towel then mix them well with the monosodium glutamate (if used) and 1 tsp of salt.

Mix the sauce ingredients, blending them together thoroughly.

Heat the peanut oil in a pan. Dip the oysters into the sauce and fry them until brown over low heat.

Serve with catsup, or prepare a dish of spiced salt by putting 1–2 tbsp of salt and 1 tsp of peppercorns in a pan over low heat until they start to brown; remove the peppercorns and keep the salt.

SIZZLING EEL

SERVES 4–6

2lb yellow eels
5 pints boiling water
3tbsp salt
⅓ cup peanut oil
2tsp fresh ginger root, chopped
½tsp pepper
2tsp Chinese yellow wine
1tbsp sugar
3tbsp dark soy sauce
⅔ cup chicken stock
2tbsp cornstarch dissolved in 1½tbsp water
2tsp spring onion, chopped
3tbsp sesame seed oil
2tsp chopped ham
1½tsp chopped coriander

Place the eels in a basin. Pour the boiling water (to which has been added 3 tbsp of salt) over them, and let them stand for 3 minutes. Take the eels out of the water and rinse them in cold water from the tap.

Separate the meat from the bone with the handle of a teaspoon, then cut the eel meat into ½×2inch strips. Set aside. Heat the oil until very hot. Add the eel, stirring, and add the chopped ginger, pepper, yellow wine, sugar, soy sauce and chicken stock. Cook for 5 minutes. Stir in the cornstarch and transfer to a plate. Make a small well in the center of the eels and put into it the chopped green onion.

Heat 3 tbsp of sesame seed oil until very hot and pour it into the "well." Add the chopped ham, garnish with coriander and serve.

◆ POULTRY ◆

DUCK WEBS IN OYSTER SAUCE

SERVES 4–6

5–6 duck webs
½lb broccoli or other greens
2–3 dried Chinese mushrooms, soaked
2 slices fresh ginger root
2 green onions
3tbsp rice wine or dry sherry
1tbsp soy sauce
½tbsp sugar
1tsp salt
1 star anise
3tbsp oyster sauce
1tsp sesame seed oil
1tbsp cornstarch
⅓ cup oil

Remove the outer skin of the duck webs; wash and clean well. Crush the ginger root and onions.

Heat up 3 tbsp of oil; toss in the crushed ginger root and onions followed by the duck webs; stir a few times; add rice wine or sherry and soy sauce. After 5 minutes or so, transfer the entire contents to a sand-pot or casserole. Add sugar, a little salt, star anise and a little stock or water. Simmer gently for 3 hours.

Just before serving, stir-fry the broccoli or greens with the dried Chinese mushrooms, a little salt and sugar. Place them on a serving dish,

DUCK WEBS IN OYSTER SAUCE

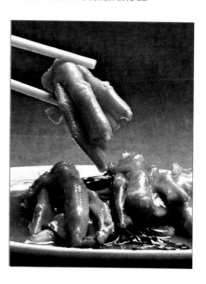

then arrange the duck webs on top of that. Meanwhile heat a little oil in a saucepan, add oyster sauce and sesame seed oil. Thicken with cornstarch mixed with a little cold water; when it is smooth, pour it over the duck webs and serve.

BRAISED FOUR TREASURES

SERVES 4–6

6 duck webs
4 duck wings
10 duck tongues
5–6 duck kidneys
½lb lard for deep-frying
1 green onion, finely chopped
1 slice fresh ginger root, finely chopped
½pt chicken stock
3tbsp rice wine or dry sherry
½tsp monosodium glutamate
1tbsp crushed bean sauce
2tsp soy sauce

Clean the duck webs in warm water and remove the outer coat of skin, then parboil for 20 minutes. Cool them in cold water and cut into small pieces about ½ inch in length.

Parboil the wings for 20 minutes. Cool them in cold water and cut into small pieces about ½ inch in length.

Clean the tongues in warm water and remove the outer layer of skin; parboil for 10 minutes, then cool in cold water.

Parboil the kidneys for 15 minutes and remove the outer layer of fat. Split each in half, cut each half in 2, then marinate in a little soy sauce. Heat up the lard in a wok or pan until smoking; fry the kidney pieces for 5 minutes or until golden, then remove and drain.

Leaving about 3 tbsp of lard in the pan, first fry the finely chopped onion and ginger root; add the chicken stock with wine or sherry, monosodium glutamate, crushed bean sauce and the remaining soy sauce, stir and add the "four treasures." Bring to a boil, then reduce the heat and simmer for about 15 minutes. When the stock is reduced by half, increase the heat to high to thicken the gravy, and serve.

MINCED DUCK WITH CROÛTONS

SERVES 4–6

4oz cooked duck meat
½ cup peas
3 slices white bread
2½ cups stock
1tsp salt
½tsp monosodium glutamate
2tsp rice wine or dry sherry
1tbsp cornstarch mixed with 1tbsp water
1tsp chicken fat for frying the bread

Finely mince the duck meat. Add it to the stock together with the peas, rice wine or sherry, salt and monosodium glutamate. Bring it to a boil over a high flame, then slowly pour in the cornstarch and water mixture. When it boils again, stir in the chicken fat, and remove.

Fry the bread cut into small cubes until they become golden and crispy; drain and place them on a soup plate, pour the minced duck all over them so they make a sizzling noise and serve at once before the fried bread croûtons become soggy.

PEKING DUCK

SERVES 6–8

3–4lb duck
1 medium cucumber
1 bunch green onions

Sauce
3–4tbsp vegetable oil
⅔ cup yellow bean paste
¼ cup sugar
1tsp sesame seed oil
Chinese pancakes

Wash and dry the duck thoroughly. Hang it up in a well-ventilated place overnight to dry the skin. Cut the cucumber into matchstick-sized shreds. Cut the green onions into similar-sized shreds.

Place the duck on a wire rack over a roasting dish. Place in a preheated oven at 400°F for 1 hour 10 minutes. It is important to make sure the oven is correctly pre-heated for a good result.

◆ POULTRY ◆

Do not open the oven door during the roasting, the duck requires no basting.

Meanwhile, to make the sauce, heat the oil in a small saucepan. When hot, add the yellow bean paste and stir over low heat for 2–3 minutes. Add the sugar and ¼ cup water and stir for another 2–3 minutes. Finally, add the sesame seed oil and stir for a further 30 seconds.

Slice off the crispy skin with a sharp knife into 1½×2 inch pieces and arrange on a heated plate. Carve the meat into similar-sized pieces and arrange on a separate heated plate. Brush each pancake with 1–1½ tsp of sauce, and add a little shredded cucumber and green onion. Place a little duck skin and meat overlapping on each pancake. Roll up, turning up

one end of the pancake to stop the filling falling out. Eat using the fingers.

AROMATIC AND CRISPY DUCK

SERVES 6–8

4–5lb duck
vegetable oil for deep-frying

Cooking sauce
2½pt good stock (see recipe)
½ cup sugar
6 slices fresh ginger root
¼ cup soy sauce
⅓ cup yellow bean paste
½ cup rice wine or dry sherry
6 pieces star anise

AROMATIC AND CRISPY DUCK

½tsp five-spice powder
¼tsp pepper

Mix the ingredients for the cooking sauce together in a large saucepan. Clean the duck thoroughly and cut in half down the backbone. Place into the liquid and submerge.

Simmer the duck gently for 2 hours. Remove from the cooking liquid and leave to cool. When required, heat the oil in a wok or deep-fryer. When hot, place the duck gently in the oil and fry for 10–11 minutes. Drain well and serve.

◆ POULTRY ◆

RED-COOKED DUCK

SERVES 6–8

4–5lb duck
3 green onions
4 slices fresh ginger root

Sauce
½tsp salt
½ cup soy sauce
3tbsp yellow bean paste
2½tsp sugar
⅓ cup rice wine or dry sherry

Wipe the duck inside and out with a damp cloth. Place breast side up in a flameproof casserole and cover with water. Bring to a boil for 10 minutes, then pour out about a quarter of the water. Cut the green onions into 1½ inch sections.

Add the ginger, green onions, salt, soy sauce and yellow bean paste to the casserole. Bring to a boil, cover and simmer for about 1 hour, turning the duck over a couple of times during the cooking. Add the sugar and sherry and continue to cook, covered, for another 45 minutes.

Serve the duck whole, or chopped through the bone into bite-sized pieces. The remaining sauce can be reduced over high heat and thickened with a small amount of cornstarch mixed with a little water, if liked. Two tsp of sesame seed oil can also be added. Pour the sauce over the whole duck or pieces of duck arranged on a large heated plate.

DUCK CARCASS SOUP

SERVES 6–8

1 duck carcass
5–7 cups water
2lb Chinese white cabbage
salt and pepper to taste

This soup is cooked and prepared in a short time. Simply boil the duck carcass in the water for 15 minutes. Cut the white cabbage into 3 inch sections and add to the soup. Continue to cook for another 15 minutes. The only seasoning required is salt

and pepper added to taste. If liked 1 tbsp dried shrimps, 2 tbsp of wine vinegar and a crumbled chicken stock cube can be included. During the cooking, keep the soup boiling. The resulting soup will be very white. If not white enough, add a couple of tbsp of milk. This soup is relatively light and is much appreciated after a rich meal.

CANTONESE ROAST DUCK

SERVES 6–8

1 duck, about 3½lb
3tsp salt

Filling
3 slices fresh ginger root
3 cloves garlic
2 green onions
¼ cup soy sauce

¾tbsp sugar
½tbsp pounded Sichuan peppercorns
⅔ cup good stock (see recipe)
1tbsp yellow bean paste
2 pieces star anise
1tbsp broken dried tangerine peel

Baste
⅔ cup boiling water
3tbsp vinegar
3tbsp soy sauce
3tbsp honey

Wash and dry the duck. Rub the duck inside and out with the salt. Hang it up to dry for 2½–3 hours. Shred the ginger. Chop the garlic. Coarsely chop the green onions. Mix the ginger, garlic and green onion together with the remaining filling ingredients. Tie the neck of the duck securely so that there is no leakage. Place the duck in a large bowl, back

◆ POULTRY ◆

ROAST DUCK WITH GARLIC

side up, and pour in the filling mixture. Sew the skin up securely. Mix the basting ingredients together.

Place the duck on a wire rack over a roasting pan filled with 1½ inches water. Brush the duck with the basting mixture and roast in a preheated oven at 400°F for 30 minutes. Brush again with the basting mixture, reduce the oven temperature to 375°F and roast for 30 minutes. Brush the duck once more, reduce the oven temperature to 350°F and roast for a further 20 minutes.

Drain the liquid from the duck into a large bowl. Place the duck on a chopping board and chop through the bones into 3×2 inch pieces. Re-assemble the duck on a heated

serving dish. Boil the liquid from inside the duck in a small pan until reduced by a quarter. Pour this sauce over the duck. Serve hot or cold.

KOU SHOA DEEP-FRIED BONELESS DUCK

SERVES 6–8

1 duck, about 4–5lb
5¾ cups cooking sauce (see Aromatic and Crispy Duck recipe)
vegetable oil for deep-frying

Batter
1 egg
6 tbsp cornstarch
3 tbsp self-rising flour

Parboil the duck in a pan of boiling water for about 5 minutes, then drain. Mix the ingredients for the batter in a bowl until smooth.

Heat the cooking sauce in a heavy pan. Add the duck and simmer gently for about 45 minutes. Remove the duck and drain thoroughly. Allow the duck to cool for 30 minutes, then remove the meat from the bones, leaving the meat in large pieces if possible. Turn the meat in the batter mixture until evenly coated. Heat the oil in a wok or deep-fryer. When hot, fry the battered duck for about 5 minutes. Drain.

Place the large duck pieces on a chopping board, cutting each piece into 3–4 pieces, and serve.

ROAST DUCK WITH GARLIC

SERVES 4–6

5–6 dried scallops
3oz garlic
9oz roast duck breast
5oz spinach
½tsp salt
3tbsp oil

Seasoning
1tbsp soy sauce
¼tsp sugar
1tbsp oyster sauce

few drops sesame seed oil
1tsp cornstarch
2tsp rice wine or dry sherry

Soak the scallops for 3–4 hours and steam for 30 minutes. Fry the garlic until brown. Cut the duck breast into 12 slices (each slice with skin attached) and arrange the meat in a big bowl (the skin to the bottom of the bowl), add a layer of scallops and finally the garlic. Steam for 45 minutes.

Fry the spinach with a little salt and oil and spread it out on a plate. Put the roast duck, scallops and garlic on top of the spinach and reserve the gravy. Boil the gravy from the bottom of the bowl in a pan. Add the seasonings and stir into a sauce. Pour the sauce over the dish and serve.

PIGEONS IN DARK SOY SAUCE

SERVES 4–6

2 pigeons or squab
4¼ cups water
1 stick cinnamon
2–3 slices licorice root
3 slices fresh ginger root
4 shallots
1 cup dark soy sauce
¾ cup light soy sauce
2 cups stock
3tbsp Chinese yellow wine
2tbsp rock sugar

Clean the pigeons. Boil 2½ pt water and blanch the pigeons for 2 minutes. Remove the pigeons from the boiling water, drain and pat dry.

Place all the remaining ingredients in a clay pot and bring to a boil. Allow to simmer over a low heat for 15 minutes before putting the pigeons into the pot to simmer in the sauce for a further 15 minutes. Let the pigeons color evenly by turning them over from time to time.

Cover the pot and turn off the heat, leaving the contents to sit for 30 minutes. Dismember the pigeons and serve with the sauce from the cooking pot.

◆ POULTRY ◆

FRIED CRISPY PIGEON

SERVES 4–6

2 young pigeons or squab

Spicy stock
½tsp dried orange peel
2 star anise
1tsp peppercorns
3 slices fresh ginger root
1 green onion
3tbsp dark soy sauce
1tsp salt
1tbsp sugar
4¼ cups water

½ tsp white vinegar
2tsp malt sugar, molasses or honey
1tsp cornstarch
2tsp water

2 cups peanut oil

Clean the pigeons. Prepare the ingredients for the spicy stock. Bring the mixture to a boil. Reduce the temperature and put the pigeons into the stock to simmer for 7 minutes. Remove and drain the pigeons and pat them dry.

Mix the vinegar, malt sugar and cornstarch with 2 tsp of water and rub the pigeons with the mixture. Hang the pigeons up to dry for 3–4 hours.

Heat the oil and fry the pigeons, turning them from side to side and basting them with the hot oil all the time to fry them evenly until the pigeons become brown, which takes about 5 minutes. Remove the pigeons and drain. Chop the pigeon in bite-sized pieces to serve.

DOUBLE-BOILED PIGEON, HAM AND BLACK MUSHROOM SOUP

SERVES 4–6

2 pigeons or squab
8oz lean pork
6 medium black mushrooms
1½oz ham
3 slices fresh ginger root
1tbsp Chinese yellow wine
2½ cups chicken stock
¼ cup oil

SALT-BAKED PIGEON

SERVES 4–6

2 pigeons or squab

Marinade
1 crushed star anise
2 cloves shallot
1tbsp green onion, shredded
1tsp fresh ginger root, shredded
2 slices licorice root
1tsp Chinese yellow wine
1tbsp dark soy sauce
1tsp ginger juice

½tsp sesame seed oil
5–6lb coarse salt
2 sheets waxed paper
2 sheets aluminum foil

Clean the pigeons and dry them with absorbent paper towels. Mix together the star anise, shallots, green

SALT-BAKED PIGEON

onion, ginger and licorice and rub the skin and the inside of the pigeons with the mixture. Blend the yellow wine, soy sauce, ginger juice and sesame seed oil together, divide it and put it into the cavities of the pigeons.

Stir-fry the coarse salt over high heat for 2 minutes. Insert about one-third of the salt into the pigeon cavities, and cover the outside of the birds with the remaining salt. Wrap each pigeon first with a piece of waxed paper and then with foil. Bake the wrapped pigeons in an oven at 350˚F for 40 minutes.

Remove the paper and foil from the pigeons and shake them free of salt. To serve, cut the pigeons into bite-sized pieces.

◆ POULTRY ◆

Clean the pigeons thoroughly. Cut out the breast meat and save it. Blanch the lean pork and pigeons in boiling water for 2 minutes and rinse under the tap for 1 minute.

Soak the black mushrooms in warm water for about 30 minutes until they have softened. Discard the stems and cut the caps into evenly-sized pieces.

Put all ingredients in a heavy pot or casserole with a lid, add the stock and an equal amount of water, and cover and steam over medium heat for 3 hours.

STIR-FRIED SUPREME OF PIGEON, BLACK MUSHROOMS AND BAMBOO SHOOTS

SERVES 4–6

5oz supreme of pigeon or squab (breast meat)

Marinade
1tsp light soy sauce
½tsp salt
½tsp sesame seed oil
¼tsp pepper
1tsp Chinese yellow wine
1tsp cornstarch

5–6 medium black mushrooms
1 cup bamboo shoots
2 cups peanut oil
1tsp salt
1tbsp stock
½tsp garlic, ground
½tsp fresh ginger root, ground

Sauce
1tbsp oyster sauce
1tsp dark soy sauce
1tbsp light soy sauce
3tbsp stock
1tsp sugar
½tsp sesame seed oil
1tbsp cornstarch
1tsp Chinese yellow wine

STIR-FRIED SUPREME OF PIGEON, BLACK MUSHROOMS AND BAMBOO SHOOTS

Cut the pigeon breasts into thin slices. Mix together the marinade ingredients and marinate the pigeon slices. Set them on one side.

Soak the black mushrooms in hot water for about 30 minutes, remove and discard the stalks and cut the caps into thin slices. Cut the bamboo shoots into slices 1½×¾×2 inch thick.

Heat a pan until very hot, add the oil and after 1 minute add the pigeon pieces. Stir to separate. Remove them from the oil and set aside. Reheat the pan and add the bamboo shoot and mushroom slices. Sauté for 1 minute. Add 1 tsp of salt and 1 tbsp of stock, cook for 2 minutes and set aside.

Heat 3 tbsp of oil in the pan. Add the garlic and ginger and when the fragrance rises add all the cooked ingredients. Stir-fry for 1 minute over high heat before adding the sauce ingredients. Stir rapidly for 15 seconds. Serve.

"THREE FAIRIES" IN THEIR OWN JUICE

SERVES 4–6

1 young chicken weighing about 1½lb
1 duckling weighing about 2½lb
½ leg of pork weighing about 2lb
2tbsp dried Chinese mushrooms, soaked
1⅓ cups bamboo shoots, sliced
2tbsp salt
5 cups duck, chicken and pork stock

Clean the chicken, duck and pork well; parboil them together in the stock (which is made from duck, chicken and pork in the first place, thus the term "in their own juice" in the name of this dish).

Place the chicken, duck and pork in a large bowl or deep dish; add soaked mushrooms, bamboo shoot slices and salt; steam vigorously for at least 2½ hours.

Obviously you will need a very large steamer for this dish. Those who would like to try it out at home can reduce the quantity of the ingredients by three-quarters.

◆ ◆ ◆

◆ MEAT ◆

tinue cooking for a while, then add monosodium glutamate and the cornstarch mixed with a little cold water; blend well and serve.

STIR-FRIED ASSORTED MEATS WITH THIN RICE-FLOUR NOODLES IN CURRY SAUCE

15oz dried rice-flour noodles (rice vermicelli)
2 eggs
4oz pork fillet
4oz shrimps, shelled and deveined
1 green bell pepper
1 red chili
½ cup peanut oil
1tbsp green onion, chopped
1tbsp fresh cilantro, chopped

Marinade
1tbsp egg white (from main recipe)
1tsp salt
2tsp cornstarch
½tsp sesame seed oil

Curry sauce
1tbsp curry paste
1tsp garlic, chopped
1tsp sugar
2tbsp light soy sauce
¼ cup chicken stock

Soak the dried rice-flour noodles in 3 pt cold water for 15 minutes. Drain and set aside.

Break 2 eggs into a mixing bowl, taking 1 tbsp of egg white for the marinade. Beat the remainder lightly and set aside. Make the marinade in a separate bowl. Cut the fillet of pork into matchstick-sized shreds and mix with half of the marinade. Set aside.

Clean the shrimps, pat them dry and mix with the other half of the marinade. Keep refrigerated for 30 minutes. Cut the green pepper and red chili into thin shreds. Set aside.

Heat 3 tbsp of oil. Stir-fry the chopped green onions until nicely browned; remove and set aside. Add the shrimps and pork, stir-frying them for 1 minute. Remove and set aside.

Make the curry sauce by heating 1½ tbsp of oil in a pan. Add the garlic

TUNG-PO PORK

SERVES 4–6

10oz fresh belly of pork
1tbsp crystal sugar
3tbsp soy sauce
3tbsp rice wine or dry sherry
2 green onions
2 slices fresh ginger root

Cut the pork into 4 equal squares. Put enough cold water in a sand-pot (or casserole) to cover the meat; bring it to a boil, then blanch the meat for 5 minutes. Take it out and rinse in cold water.

Discard the water in which the meat has been blanched; place a bamboo rack at the bottom of the pot, then place the meat skin side down in it; add crystal sugar, soy sauce and rice wine or sherry. Place the onions and ginger root on top; seal the lid tightly with flour and water paste and cook gently for at least 2 hours or until tender. Discard the ginger root and onions and transfer the meat into a bowl, skin

STIR-FRIED ASSORTED MEATS WITH THIN RICE-FLOUR NOODLES IN CURRY SAUCE

side up this time, with 3 pieces on the bottom layer and 1 piece on top. Pour the juice over them, cover and steam vigorously for at least 2 hours before serving.

HAM AND BROAD BEANS

SERVES 4–6

4oz best ham
½lb fresh or thawed frozen lima beans
3tbsp lard
1tsp salt
¼tsp monosodium glutamate
1tsp sugar
½tsp cornstarch
⅓ cup stock

Use the young, tender broad beans when in season. Peel off the skin. Dice the ham into small cubes.

Warm up the lard and stir-fry the lima beans and ham at the same time. Add sugar, salt and stock, con-

◆ MEAT ◆

and curry paste. When the aroma rises, add the sugar, soy sauce and chicken stock. Bring to a boil, transfer to a bowl and set aside.

Heat ¼ cup of oil in a pan until very hot. Add the rice noodles and stir, turning the noodles over with the help of chopsticks. Stir-fry over a high heat for 3 minutes. Transfer to a plate and set aside.

Add 1 tbsp of oil to the pan. Fry the beaten egg until partly set and add the green pepper and red chili. Keep stirring.

Return the shrimps and pork, and stir. Add the rice noodles to the pan and the curry sauce, stirring vigorously over high heat for 3 minutes. Transfer to a plate, place the fried green onion and chopped cilantro on top and serve.

BEEF AND BLACK MUSHROOMS

SERVES 4–6

4oz pork fat
1¼lb ground beef
⅔ cup stock
1tbsp cornstarch
1tsp sesame seed oil
2½tsp salt
12 small black mushrooms
1tsp sugar
1tbsp peanut oil

Cut the pork fat into tiny cubes and blanch the pieces in boiling water for 1 minute. Rinse under the tap. Put the pork fat, ground beef, stock, cornstarch, sesame seed oil and 1½ tsp of salt in a mixing bowl and stir in one direction only, with a fork until the mixture becomes sticky.

Soak the black mushrooms in hot water for 30 minutes, remove and discard the stems and place the caps in a bowl. Add 1 tsp of salt, the sugar and peanut oil and mix well. Steam the mushrooms over medium heat for 5 minutes and set aside.

Divide the beef into 12 portions, molding each portion into an egg shape and place 1 mushroom on top of each "egg." Use 6 small dishes and

place 2 of the beef and mushroom "eggs" in each dish. Steam over high heat for 5 minutes and serve.

SHREDDED BEEF WITH CELERY

SERVES 4–6

½lb beef steak
2oz celery
2oz leek or green onion
2 slices fresh ginger root
1tbsp chili paste
2tbsp soy sauce
½tsp salt
1tsp sugar
1tbsp rice wine or dry sherry
1tsp vinegar
¼ cup oil

Shred the beef into thin matchstick-sized strips. Shred the celery and leeks the same size (Chinese leeks are a cross between the Western leek and green onion with thin skin and green foliage). Peel the ginger root and cut it into thin shreds.

Heat up the wok or pan and put in the oil. When it start to smoke, stir-fry the beef for a short while, add the chili paste, blend well, then add the celery, leek and ginger root, followed by the soy sauce, salt, sugar and wine. Stir for 1–2 minutes, then add vinegar and serve.

SESAME BEEF

SERVES 4–6

11oz rump steak
1tbsp white sesame seeds
2½ cups peanut oil

Marinade
1tbsp light soy sauce
1tsp dark soy sauce
1tsp sugar
1tsp sesame seed oil
1tsp Chinese yellow wine

Cut the steak into thin slices 1×2×⅛ inch. Prepare the marinade and mix the beef slices with it. Set aside. Sauté sesame seeds in a pan over low heat until nicely golden in color. Set aside.

Heat the peanut oil. Add the beef, reduce the heat to medium and fry for 3 minutes. Remove the meat and bring oil back to a high temperature. Return the beef to the oil and fry for a further 30 seconds.

Drain the beef and pat it with absorbent paper towels before transferring it to a serving dish. Sprinkle it with sesame seeds and serve.

SHREDDED BEEF WITH CELERY

◆ MEAT ◆

RED-COOKED OXTAIL

SERVES 4–6

2 cloves garlic
5–6lb oxtail (ask butcher to cut into sections)
2–3 young carrots
3 slices fresh ginger root
1tsp salt
½ cup soy sauce
2tbsp hoisin sauce
⅓ cup rice wine or dry sherry
⅔ cup good stock
2tsp sugar
3tbsp peas (optional)

Crush the garlic. Clean the oxtail. Cut the carrots slantwise into ¼ inch slices. Blanch the oxtail for 3–4 minutes in a pan of boiling water. Drain and place in a heavy saucepan or flameproof casserole with the garlic, ginger, salt, soy sauce, hoisin sauce and carrots. Add 3¾ cups of water.

Bring the contents of the pan to a boil, cover and simmer very gently for 1½ hours. Turn the contents every 30 minutes. Add the wine or sherry, stock and sugar and continue to simmer gently for a further 1 hour, turning the contents after 30 minutes. Add the peas 10 minutes before the end of the cooking time. (If cooked in the oven, cook at 300°F for 3 hours.)

QUICK-FRIED SHREDDED BEEF WITH GINGER AND ONIONS

SERVES 5–6

1lb beef steak, eg, rump or fillet
1tsp salt
pepper to taste
2tbsp cornstarch
1 egg white
3 medium onions
3 slices fresh ginger root
⅓ cup vegetable oil
2tbsp lard
3tbsp soy sauce
1tbsp sugar
¼ cup good stock
2tbsp rice wine or dry sherry
2tsp cornstarch blended with 3tbsp water

Using a very sharp knife, cut the beef into thin slices, then cut again into matchstick-sized shreds. Sprinkle with the salt and pepper. Toss in the 2 tbsp of cornstarch and coat in the egg white. Peel and thinly slice the onions. Shred the ginger.

Heat the oil in a wok or skillet. When hot, stir-fry the beef over high heat for 1½ minutes. Remove and set aside. Add the lard to the pan. When hot, stir-fry the ginger and onions over high heat for 1½ minutes. Add the soy sauce, sugar and stock and stir together for 30 seconds. Return the beef, add the wine or sherry and blended cornstarch and continue to stir-fry for 30 seconds.

SLICED BEEF IN BLACK BEAN AND CHILI SAUCE

SERVES 4–6

1lb beef steak, eg, rump, fillet or sirloin
¼tsp salt
pepper to taste
3tbsp cornstarch
1 egg white
⅓ cup vegetable oil

Sauce
1 medium onion
2 dried chilies
1 small red bell pepper
1 small green bell pepper
2tbsp salted black beans
1tbsp lard
¼ cup good stock
1tbsp rice wine or dry sherry
1tbsp soy sauce
½tbsp cornstarch blended with 3tbsp water

Cut the beef into thin slices and rub evenly with salt and pepper. Toss in the cornstarch and coat in the egg white. Peel and thinly slice the onion. Finely chop the chilies. Cut the red and green peppers into 1 inch pieces. Soak the black beans in ⅓ cup of cold water for 3 minutes, then drain.

Heat the oil in a wok or skillet. When hot, stir-fry the beef over high heat for 1 minute. Remove and set aside. Add the lard to the pan. When hot, stir-fry the onion, black beans, chilies and peppers. Mash the softened black beans with a metal spoon against the edge of the wok or pan. Stir in the stock, rice wine or sherry and soy sauce over high heat. Return the beef to the pan and mix well. Finally, add the blended cornstarch to thicken the sauce. Stir all the ingredients for a further 30 seconds.

CANTONESE STIR-FRIED BEEF IN OYSTER SAUCE

SERVES 4–6

1lb beef steak, eg, rump or fillet
1tsp salt
pepper to taste
2tbsp cornstarch
1 egg white
3 slices fresh ginger root
4oz snow peas or 3–4 green onions
⅓ cup vegetable oil
1tsp lard
2tbsp good stock
1tbsp soy sauce
2tbsp oyster sauce
1tbsp rice wine or dry sherry

Cut the beef into thin strips and mix with the salt and pepper. Toss in the cornstarch and coat in the egg white. Shred the ginger. Cut each snow pea slantwise in half or cut the green onions slantwise in 1½ inch sections.

Heat the oil in a wok or skillet. When hot, stir-fry the ginger in the oil to flavor. Add the beef and stir-fry over high heat for about 1 minute. Remove and set aside. Add the lard to the pan. When hot, stir-fry the snow peas or green onions for 1–2 minutes. Add the stock and soy sauce, and continue to stir-fry for 30 seconds. Return the beef to the pan, add the oyster sauce and wine or sherry and stir-fry over high heat for 30 seconds.

CANTONESE STIR-FRIED BEEF IN OYSTER SAUCE

◆ MEAT ◆

◆ MEAT ◆

LAMB IN SWEET AND SOUR SAUCE

SERVES 4–6

½lb lamb fillet
2 slices fresh ginger root
1tbsp crushed yellow bean sauce
3tbsp cornstarch
1½tbsp soy sauce
1tbsp rice wine or dry sherry
1tbsp vinegar
3tbsp sugar
oil for deep-frying
½tbsp chicken fat or sesame seed oil

Thinly slice the lamb fillet and finely chop the ginger root. Mix the lamb with ½ tbsp of cornstarch with soy sauce, rice wine or sherry, vinegar, sugar and the finely chopped ginger root.

Heat up the oil in a wok or pan, fry the lamb slices for about 15 seconds and stir to separate them. When they turn pale, scoop them out and return the lamb slices to the wok over a high heat. Add the sauce mixture, stir and blend well for about 1 minute; add chicken fat or sesame seed oil, stir a few more times, then serve.

RINSED LAMB IN FIREPOT

If you cannot obtain a Chinese firepot, sometimes known as a chafing pot, then use a fondue or an electrically heated pan on the table.

SERVES 4–6

3–3½lb boned shoulder, loin or leg of lamb
1lb Chinese cabbage
1lb spinach
2 cakes tofu (fresh or frozen)
4oz transparent noodles
5½–6 pints water or stock

Sauce
green onions, finely chopped
garlic and fresh ginger root
soy sauce
rice wine or dry sherry
hoisin sauce
vinegar
sugar
chili sauce and sesame seed oil

Cut the lamb into fairly large but very, very thin slices — you will find that it is much easier to do this if the meat is half-frozen.

Wash and cut the cabbage and spinach into biggish pieces; cut each cake of the tofu into 10 to 12 slices; soak the transparent noodles in warm water for a few minutes, then drain.

Arrange the cabbage, spinach, tofu, transparent noodles and the meat in separate serving dishes and place them on the table with the firepot in the middle.

While waiting for the water or stock to boil in the moat of the firepot, each diner prepares his or her sauce by mixing a little of the various ingredients in individual sauce dishes according to his or her own taste.

◆ MEAT ◆

When the water or stock is boiling vigorously, pick up a piece of lamb with chopsticks and dip it in the water to cook it, occasionally dunking it as if rinsing — hence the name of the dish.

Depending on the thickness and cut of the meat, it should not take more than 20–30 seconds to cook, otherwise it will be too tough. Then dip the cooked meat in the sauce mixture and eat it.

Start adding the vegetables to the moat and eat them with the meat. As the cooking progresses, the pot is recharged with charcoal; the remaining water or stock is put in the moat, and the contents get tastier and tastier.

When all the meat is eaten, put the rest of the vegetables into the moat, to make a delicious soup.

DICED LAMB WITH SPRING ONIONS

SERVES 4–6

½lb lamb fillet
½lb green onions
2tbsp cornstarch
1tsp salt
2tsp soy sauce
1 eggwhite
½tbsp rice wine or dry sherry
oil for deep-frying
1tsp sesame seed oil

Dice the lamb into ½ inch cubes, marinate with ½ tsp of salt, egg white and ¾ tbsp of cornstarch. Cut the onions into ½ inch lengths.

Heat about 2½ cups oil in a wok. Before the oil gets too hot, add the lamb cubes, separate them with chopsticks or a fork, then scoop them out and drain.

Pour off the excess oil and leave about 3 tbsp in the wok. Put in the onions followed by the lamb cubes, salt, soy sauce, rice wine or sherry and remaining cornstarch; stir for 1–2 minutes; add the sesame seed oil, stir a few more times, then serve.

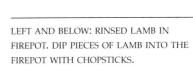

LEFT AND BELOW: RINSED LAMB IN FIREPOT. DIP PIECES OF LAMB INTO THE FIREPOT WITH CHOPSTICKS.

◆ MEAT ◆

LONG-STEAMED WINE-SOAKED LAMB

SERVES 7–8

1½lb leg of lamb
12oz turnips
1 dried tangerine peel
2 cups white wine
⅔ cup rice wine or dry sherry
1¼ cups water
5 slices fresh ginger root
1½tsp salt

Cut the lamb into 1 inch cubes. Cut the turnips into similar-sized cubes. Parboil the lamb and turnips in a pan of water for about 3 minutes, then drain. Soak the tangerine peel in hot water for 5 minutes, then drain and break into small pieces.

Put the lamb and turnip into a large heavy flameproof casserole with the white wine, rice wine or sherry, water, ginger, salt and tangerine peel. Bring to a boil, then place the casserole, covered, in a steamer and steam for 3 hours. If you do not have a large enough steamer, it is possible to cook the dish by placing the casserole into a pan containing 2 inches of water (a roasting pan will do) and then double boil the casserole for the same amount of time. The dish is brought to the table and diners serve themselves.

MUSLIM LONG-SIMMERED LAMB

SERVES 8–10

4–5lb neck of lamb
3 medium onions
2 dried chilies
4 slices fresh ginger root
4 cloves garlic
3¾ pints water
3tsp salt

Dip sauce
⅔ cup soy sauce
3tbsp garlic, finely chopped
3tbsp fresh ginger root, finely chopped
3tbsp green onions, finely chopped
3tbsp fresh cilantro, finely chopped
2tbsp prepared English mustard
2tbsp wine vinegar
¼ cup rice wine or dry sherry
1tbsp sesame seed oil
1tbsp vegetable oil

Cut the lamb into 2×1×¼ inch thick slices. Par-boil in a pan of water for 3 minutes, then drain. Peel and slice the onions. Shred the chilies, discarding the seeds. Shred the ginger. Crush the garlic.

Place the lamb in a heavy flameproof casserole with a lid. Add the water, salt, onion, ginger, garlic and chili. Bring to a boil, reduce the heat and simmer slowly for 3 hours, turning the contents every 30 minutes. Add more water if the sauce becomes too thick. Meanwhile, mix the dip sauce ingredients together. Serve the casserole at the table. Eat the lamb with the dip sauce.

AROMATIC MUTTON

SERVES 4–6

1½lb mutton fillet
11oz leeks
1¾ cup peanut oil
1tsp garlic, chopped
1tsp Chinese yellow wine

Marinade
1tbsp light soy sauce
1tsp dark soy sauce
1tsp sesame seed oil
2tsp Chinese yellow wine
1tbsp cornstarch

Cut the mutton fillet into thin slices. Mix together the marinade ingredients, add the mutton slices and set to one side. Cut the leek into thin slices and set aside.

Heat a pan until it is very hot and add the oil. Heat the oil until it is warm and add the mutton (reserving the marinade in a separate bowl) and stir to separate. Remove, drain and set aside.

Heat 3 tbsp of oil in the pan and add the chopped garlic and leek, stir and cook over a very high heat for 1 minute.

Return the mutton to the pan, stirring well. Add the reserved marinade, stirring vigorously over a very high heat for 15 seconds. Finally, add the Chinese yellow wine, stir for another 10 seconds and serve.

TUNG-PO MUTTON

SERVES 4–6

½lb stewing mutton
4oz potato
4oz carrot
3tbsp soy sauce
1tbsp sugar
2 green onions
1 slice fresh ginger root
1 clove garlic, crushed
1tsp five-spice powder
¼ cup rice wine or dry sherry
½tsp Sichuan pepper
oil for deep-frying

Cut the mutton into 1 inch cubes, then score one side of each square halfway down. Peel the potato and carrot and cut them the same size and shape as the mutton.

Heat up quite a lot of oil in a wok or deep-fryer. When it is smoking, deep-fry the mutton for 5–6 seconds or until it turns golden; scoop out and drain, then fry the potato and carrot, also until golden.

Place the mutton in a pot or casserole, cover the meat with cold water, add soy sauce, sugar, onions, ginger root, garlic, pepper, five-spice powder and rice wine or sherry, and bring it to a boil. Then reduce the heat and simmer for 2–3 hours; add potato and carrot, cook together for about 5 minutes and serve.

PORK VARIETY MEATS (OFFAL) IN CASSEROLE

SERVES 6–8

pigs' heart, liver, tripe, kidneys and tongue
½lb Chinese cabbage (or spinach)
⅔ cup bamboo shoots
3–4 dried Chinese mushrooms

◆ MEAT ◆

1 slice fresh ginger root
1 green onion
1tbsp rice wine or dry sherry
salt to taste

The tripe should be cleaned thoroughly, parboiled for about 10 minutes, and then marinated in a little salt and vinegar for 2 minutes. After that, rinse well in clean, cold water.

First place the tripe on the bottom of a big pot or casserole, followed by the tongue and heart, and finally the kidneys and liver. Add enough cold water to cover, then bring it to a rapid boil. Skim off the impurities floating on the surface, then reduce

the heat and let it simmer with a lid on.

After simmering for 30 minutes, remove the liver and kidneys; next remove the tongue and heart, after about an hour's cooking. The tripe will have to be cooked for 2 hours or more, so take it out when it is well done. Reserve the stock in which the meat has been cooked.

Cut the tripe and heart into small chunks, the tongue, kidneys and liver into slices.

Wash the cabbage or spinach in cold water and cut it into small pieces. Soak the dried mushrooms in warm water for about 20 minutes, then remove the hard stalks and cut

TUNG-PO MUTTON

them into small pieces together with the bamboo shoots.

Place the cabbage or spinach on the bottom of a pot or casserole, then put the tripe, heart, tongue, kidneys and liver over it, followed by the bamboo shoots and dried Chinese mushrooms; finally, add the ginger root and onions, salt and rice wine or sherry. Add enough of the stock in which the meats have been cooked to cover the entire contents, cover with a tightly fitting lid and bring to a rapid boil. To serve, bring the casserole or pot to the table.

◆ MEAT ◆

BRAISED TRIPE

SERVES 4–6

2lb tripe
salt
2 slices fresh ginger root
2 green onions
3tbsp rice wine or dry sherry
⅓ cup soy sauce
1tbsp sugar
1tsp five-spice powder
3tbsp oil
1tsp sesame seed oil

Wash the tripe thoroughly, rub both sides with the salt several times and rinse well. Blanch it in boiling water for 20 minutes. Drain and discard the water.

Heat oil, brown the tripe lightly, add ginger root, onions, rice wine or sherry, soy sauce, sugar and five-spice powder. Add 5 cups water and bring it to a boil, reduce heat and simmer gently under cover for 2 hours.

Remove the tripe and cut into small slices; garnish with sesame seed oil and serve hot or cold.

SHREDDED KIDNEYS IN WINE SAUCE

SERVES 4–6

1lb pigs' kidneys
5–6 dried Chinese mushrooms
⅓ cup bamboo shoots
½ cup green cabbage heart or broccoli
1½tbsp rice wine or dry sherry
1tsp salt
1tbsp soy sauce
½tsp monosodium glutamate
1 slice fresh ginger root, 1 green onion,
chopped and freshly ground pepper, to garnish

Peel off the thin white skin covering the kidneys, split them in half lengthwise and discard the white parts in the middle. Shred each half into thin slices and soak them in cold water for an hour or so.

Soak the mushrooms in warm water for 20 minutes, squeeze dry and discard the hard stalks, then cut them into thin shreds. Cut the bamboo shoots and greens into thin shreds, blanch them in boiling water for a few minutes (if using canned bamboo shoots this will be unnecessary as they have already been cooked), then drain and mix them with 1 tsp of salt.

POACHED KIDNEY AND LIVER WITH GREEN ONION AND GINGER

◆ MEAT ◆

Parboil the kidneys in about 4¼ cups boiling water for a few minutes, scoop them out, rinse in cold water and drain. Place them in a bowl, add the bamboo shoots, mushrooms, cabbage, soy sauce, rice wine or sherry and monosodium glutamate; mix well and marinate for 20 minutes or so. Arrange the contents on a serving plate and garnish.

POACHED KIDNEY AND LIVER WITH GREEN ONION AND GINGER

SERVES 4–6

8oz pigs' kidney
8oz pigs' liver
⅓ cup peanut oil
2 cups boiling water
1tbsp salt
3tbsp fresh ginger root, shredded
5tbsp green onion, shredded

Sauce
⅔ cup chicken stock
2tsp dark soy sauce
2tbsp light soy sauce
1tsp sugar
1tsp sesame seed oil
2tsp Chinese yellow wine

Slit open the kidney and remove the membrane and gristle. Cut the kidney into slices ⅛ inch thick and soak in cold water. Set aside.

Cut the liver into slices ⅛in thick. Soak in cold water and set aside. Heat 3 tbsp of oil in a pan, add the boiling water, bring to a boil and add the salt. Add the kidney to the boiling water. Poach for 2 minutes, remove and drain. Bring the water to a boil again and add the liver. Poach for 2 minutes, remove and drain. Bring the water to a boil for the third time. Return the kidney and liver and add the shredded ginger and green onion. Turn off the heat and allow the ingredients to stand in the hot water for 4–5 minutes. Remove and drain.

In the meantime prepare the sauce. Heat 3 tbsp of oil in a pan, add the sauce ingredients and bring to a boil.

Transfer the poached kidney, liver, ginger and spring onion to a serving dish, pour the sauce on top and serve.

FIVE-FRAGRANT KIDNEY SLICES

SERVES 4–6

½lb pigs' kidneys
1tsp red coloring
1½ cups chicken stock
1tbsp soy sauce
1tbsp rice wine or dry sherry
1 slice fresh ginger root
1tsp salt
1tsp five-spice powder
1 green onion

Place the kidneys in cold water in a pan; bring to a boil; skim off any impurities floating on the surface; reduce heat and simmer for 30 minutes. Remove and drain.

Place the kidneys in fresh cold water (just enough to cover), add the

FIVE-FRAGRANT KIDNEY SLICES

red coloring (if Chinese red-powder is unobtainable, then use a little cochineal). Bring to a boil, then remove and rinse in cold water and drain.

Put the chicken stock in a pot or pan; add the soy sauce, wine or sherry, ginger root, onion, salt, five-spice powder and the kidneys. Boil for 5 minutes, then place the kidneys with the stock in a large bowl to cool. This will take 5–6 hours.

Take the kidneys out and cut them into as thin slices as you possibly can. Place the unevenly cut slices in the middle of a plate to make a pile, then neatly arrange the rest of the slices all the way around it in 2 or 3 layers like the petals of an opened flower. Then through a strainer pour a little of the juice in which the kidneys have been cooking over the "flower" but be careful not to disturb the beautiful "petals." Serve cold as an hors d'oeuvre.

◆ DESSERTS AND SNACKS ◆

SPRING ROLL WRAPPERS

MAKES APPROXIMATELY 12

1 egg
1½ cups flour
½tsp salt
½ cup water
cornstarch

Lightly beat the egg. Sift the flour and salt into a large bowl. Make a well in the center and mix the beaten egg and water into the flour. Stir with a wooden spoon to form a smooth dough. Place the dough on a floured board and knead it for 10 minutes until smooth. Cover with a damp cloth and leave to rest for about 30 minutes. Roll the dough into a 12 inch sausage, then cut into 1½ inch pieces. Dust with cornstarch and flatten with the palm of your hand. Roll as thinly as possible, then trim to 6×7 inch rectangles. Dust with cornstarch and stack them up.

SPRING ROLL FILLINGS

SERVES 6–8

12oz lean pork or chicken meat
2 slices fresh ginger root
¼ cup drained, canned bamboo shoots
8 medium dried Chinese mushrooms
2 green onions
¼ cup vegetable oil
1tsp salt
2tbsp soy sauce
2 cups bean sprouts
1tbsp cornstarch blended with 2tbsp water
beaten egg for sealing
vegetable oil for deep-frying

Cut the pork or chicken into matchstick-sized shreds. Cut the ginger and bamboo shoots into similar or finer shreds. Soak the dried mushrooms in hot water to cover for 25 minutes. Drain and discard the tough stalks. Cut the mushroom caps into fine shreds. Divide the green onions lengthwise in half, then cut into ½ inch sections.

Heat the 3 tbsp of oil in a wok or skillet. When hot, stir-fry the ginger, salt, mushrooms and shredded meat over high heat for 1¼ minutes. Add all the other ingredients, except the cornstarch, and stir-fry for 1 minute. Pour in the blended cornstarch, stir and turn for another 30 seconds. Remove from the heat and cool before using as a filling.

Take 2 tbsp of filling and spread across each pancake just below the center. Fold the pancake up from the bottom by raising the lower corner to fold over the filling. Roll the filling over once, and bring in the 2 corners from the side to overlap each other. Finally fold the top flap down, sealing with a little beaten egg. Stack the spring rolls as you make them, placing them so that the weight of the pancake rests on the flap that has just been sealed.

Fry the pancakes soon after they have been made, as otherwise they may become soggy. Heat the oil in a wok or deep-fryer. When hot, fry not more than 5–6 pancakes at a time for 3¾–4½ minutes until golden-brown and crispy. Once fried, they can be kept crispy in the oven for up to 30 minutes. Or store them in the refrigerator for a day after an initial frying of 2½ minutes, then re-fry them for 3 minutes when required.

SESAME SHRIMP ON TOAST

SERVES 7–8

8oz peeled shrimp
⅓ cup pork fat
1tsp salt
pepper to taste
½tsp ground ginger
1tbsp dry sherry or white wine
1½tbsp green onion, finely chopped
1 egg white
2tsp cornstarch
6 slices bread
⅓ cup sesame seeds
vegetable oil for deep-frying

Chop and mix the shrimp and pork fat into a paste in a bowl. Add the salt, pepper, ginger, sherry or wine, green onion, egg white and cornstarch. Mix together thoroughly. Spread the mixture very thickly on the top of the slices of bread. Spread the sesame seeds evenly over the surface of a large plate or a small tray. Place each piece of bread, spread side down, on the sesame seeds. Press gently so that each slice has a good coating of seeds.

Heat the oil in a wok or deep-fryer. When hot, fry the slices of bread, spread-side down (only 2–3 slices of bread can be fried at a time) for 2½ minutes. Turn over and fry for a further 1½ minutes. Drain on absorbent paper towels.

When all the slices of bread have been fried and drained, place each piece of bread on a chopping board, cut off and discard the crusts. Cut the coated and fried bread slices into 6 rectangular pieces (the size of fish fingers) or into 4 triangles. Arrange them on a heated serving dish and serve hot.

SA CHI MA

¾ cup flour
2tsp baking powder
3 eggs
1 cup sugar
¾ cup maltose or honey
1 cup water
oil for deep-frying

Sift flour and baking powder onto a pastry board. Spread to form a hollow in the center; add eggs, blend well. Then knead the dough thoroughly until it is smooth.

Roll the dough with a rolling pin until it is like a big pancake about ⅛ inch in thickness. Cut it into 2-inch long thin strips; dust strips with flour so they won't stick.

Heat up the oil and deep-fry the thin strips in batches for 45 seconds until light golden. Remove. Drain.

Place the sugar, maltose or honey and water in a saucepan; bring it to a boil over high heat; simmer and stir until the mixture is like syrup. Add the thin strips and mix thoroughly until each strip is coated with syrup. Turn it out into a pre-greased cake pan and press to form one big piece. When cool, cut it into squares with a sharp knife.

SPRING ONION PANCAKES

SERVES 5–6   *Makes 10 pancakes*

3 large green onions   *Too sticky*
2⅓ cups all-purpose flour
1¼ cups boiling water
⅓ cup lard
6tbsp cold water
1½tbsp large grain sea salt

Coarsely chop the green onions. Sift the flour into a large bowl. Slowly add the boiling water and 1 tbsp of the lard. Stir with a fork or a pair of chopsticks for 3 minutes. Mix in the cold water and knead for 2 minutes. Leave the dough to stand for 30 minutes. Form and roll the dough into a long roll and cut into 10 equal sections. Roll each piece into a ball and press the ball into a flat pancake. Sprinkle the pancake evenly with salt and chopped green onion. Fold it up from the sides to form a ball again, then press again into a pancake.

Heat the remaining lard in a wok or skillet. When hot, spread the pancake evenly over the pan and fry over low heat for 2½ minutes on either side, until golden brown.

TOFFEE BANANAS

SERVES 4

4 bananas, peeled
1 egg
3tbsp all-purpose flour
oil for deep-frying
⅓ cup sugar
1tbsp cold water

Cut the bananas in half lengthwise and then cut each half into 2 crosswise.

Beat the egg, add the flour and mix well to make a smooth batter.

Heat the oil in a wok or deep-fryer. Coat each piece of banana with batter and deep-fry until golden. Remove and drain.

Pour off excess oil leaving about 1 tbsp of oil in the wok. Add sugar and water and stir over medium heat. When the sugar has caramelized, add the hot banana pieces. Coat well and remove. Dip hot bananas in cold water to harden the toffee and serve.

PLUM-BLOSSOM AND SNOW COMPETING FOR SPRING

SERVES 4

2 apples
2 bananas
2 eggs
½ cup sugar
¼ cup milk
¼ cup cornstarch
3tbsp water

Skin and remove the cores of the apples, then cut the apples and bananas into thin slices. Arrange them in alternate layers on an ovenproof dish. Separate the yolks from the whites and mix the yolks with the sugar, milk, water and cornstarch. Heat this mixture over a gentle heat until smooth, then pour it over the apple and banana.

Beat the egg whites, pour on top of the yolk mixture and bake in a hot oven (425˚F) for about 5 minutes. Serve hot or cold.

SPRING ROLLS

◆ DESSERTS AND SNACKS ◆

RED BEAN PASTE PANCAKES

½ cup all-purpose flour
½ cup boiling water
1 egg
¼ cup oil
4–5tbsp sweetened red bean paste or chestnut purée

Sift the flour into a mixing bowl and very gently pour in the boiling water. Add about 1 tsp of oil and the beaten egg. Knead the mixture into a firm dough and then divide it into 2 equal portions. Roll out each portion into a long "sausage" on a lightly floured surface and cut it into 4–6 pieces. Using the palm of your hand, press

each piece into a flat pancake. On a lightly floured surface, flatten each pancake into a 6 inch circle with a rolling pin and roll gently.

Place an ungreased skillet on high heat. When hot, reduce the heat to low and place one pancake at a time in the pan. Turn it over when little brown spots appear on the underside. Remove and keep under a damp cloth until you have finished making all the pancakes.

Spread about 2 tbsp of red bean paste or chestnut purée over about 80 per cent of the pancake surface and roll it over 3 or 4 times to form a flattened roll.

Heat the oil in a skillet and shallow-fry the pancakes until

THOUSAND-LAYER CAKES

golden-brown, turning over once. Cut each pancake into 3–4 pieces and serve hot or cold.

WON'T STICK THREE WAYS

SERVES 4–6

5 egg yolks
2tbsp cornstarch
5tbsp water
½ cup sugar
¼ cup lard

Beat the egg yolks, add sugar, cornstarch and water, blend well.

◆ DESSERTS AND SNACKS ◆

Heat the lard in a skillet over high heat, tilt the pan so that the entire surface is covered by lard, then pour the excess lard (about half) into a jug for later use. Reduce the heat to moderate, pour the egg mixture into the pan, stir and scramble for about 2 minutes and add the remaining lard from the jug little by little, stirring and scrambling all the time until the eggs become bright golden, then serve.

THOUSAND-LAYER CAKES

5¼ cups flour
2tsp dried yeast
1½ cups warm water
¾ cup sugar
¼ cup lard
¼ cup walnuts, crushed

Sift the flour into a mixing bowl and add the sugar; dissolve the yeast in warm water and slowly pour it in, then knead it well for 5 minutes. Cover the dough with a damp cloth and let it stand for 3 hours or until it doubles in volume.

Now divide the dough into 3 equal portions, then roll out each portion into a thin rectangle measuring about 1 ft×8 inches. Spread some lard and sprinkle a few chopped walnut pieces on the surface of one portion, and place another one on top to make a "sandwich." Then spread some lard and walnut pieces on top of the sandwich, and place the third portion on top to form a double-decker sandwich.

Now roll this sandwich flat until it measures roughly 2½×1 ft. Spread some lard and walnuts over two-thirds of the surface of the dough, then fold one-third over to cover the middle section and spread lard and walnuts on top of that, then fold the other one-third over.

Turn the dough around so that the folded edge faces you. Repeat the rolling, spreading and folding twice more so that you end up with the dough measuring roughly 1 ft×8

inch again but with 81 layers.

Let it stand for 30 minutes, then place it on a wet cloth in a steamer and steam over boiling water for 50–60 minutes.

Remove and let it cool a little, then cut the cake into squares or diamonds before serving.

TOFFEE APPLES

SERVES 4

3 apples
1tbsp lemon juice
¾ cup cornstarch
3tbsp sesame seeds
1 cup ice cubes
2½ cups iced water
2 cups peanut oil
1½ cups sugar
1tsp vinegar

Peel and core the apples and cut each into 6 pieces. Cut each piece into 3. Sprinkle lemon juice over the apples immediately to prevent discoloration. Coat the apple pieces with cornstarch and set them aside. Sauté

TOFFEE APPLES

the sesame seeds in a pan over a low heat. Set aside.

rub a serving plate with oil and set it aside. Place the ice cubes and iced water in a bowl and set them aside.

Heat the oil and fry the apple for 10 minutes until nicely golden. Remove, drain and set aside. In another pan bring 1½ cups water to a vigorous boil. Add the sugar, stirring until it starts to caramelize, then add the vinegar and stir. Add the apple pieces until they are evenly coated with syrup. Sprinkle sesame seeds over the apples and transfer them to a plate.

Dip the syrup-coated apple pieces into the iced water. Remove immediately or when the syrup hardens and becomes brittle. It is worth practising this recipe a few times to achieve the correct contrast between the brittle, ice-cold coating of caramelized sugar and the hot, tender apple center.

◆ ◆ ◆